Foreword

The creation of new knowledge is one of the principal purposes of today's universities. The discovery of new truths in advertising, as in any field, is the product of long and painstaking thought and inquiry. However, such truths are of vital concern to all of us who teach or practice advertising in today's complex world.

The universities are perhaps uniquely equipped to bring together leading scholars, researchers, and executives to examine the state of advertising—or for that matter, of any such professional field. The retirement of C. H. Sandage, a pioneer in advertising theory and research, provided a highly appropriate occasion for bringing together some of the leaders in advertising thought. A generous gift from publisher Richard D. Irwin helped make the symposium financially possible. The people we invited to prepare papers were naturally quite busy with their research, their teaching, or their administrative duties; we were delighted, however, at how willing they were to devote the many hours it takes to prepare such original contributions as these and to come to Allerton House at the University of Illinois to deliver them.

All members of the Department of Advertising faculty and staff put in many overtime hours to bring the C. H. Sandage Symposium to fruition. However, the special contributions of several members of the faculty should be pointed out. First of all, Arnold Barban supervised the planning and execution of the program itself. Ronald H. Pyszka chaired the arrangements committee that handled the countless details involved in putting on a two-day symposium of this sort. Jack W. Kitson was in charge of invitations and publicity. Nugent Wedding planned and supervised the banquet honoring C. H. Sandage. And Hugh W. Sargent is responsible for editing the papers and writing the introduction to this volume.

S. WATSON DUNN, *Head*
Department of Advertising
University of Illinois

CHARLES H. SANDAGE

Frontiers of Advertising Theory and Research

Frontiers of Advertising Theory and Research

A Symposium Honoring C. H. Sandage

Edited by Hugh W. Sargent

Pacific Books, Publishers Palo Alto, California

International Standard Book Number 0–87015–192–4

Library of Congress Catalog Card Number 71–88377

Printed and bound in the United States of America

PACIFIC BOOKS, PUBLISHERS
P.O. BOX 558, PALO ALTO, CALIFORNIA 94302

A Biographical Note

Dr. Charles H. Sandage, who retired as professor of advertising at the University of Illinois in 1968, has the distinction of having trained more professors of advertising than any other person in this country.

In his twenty-two years at the University of Illinois, Dr. Sandage created and developed a distinguished professional program of advertising education, both undergraduate and graduate. His far-ranging academic and professional activities helped him design a curriculum well-balanced between theoretical and practical. He also was instrumental in establishing the James Webb Young Fund, which provides financial assistance to graduate students in the Department of Advertising, a department he headed from 1946 to 1966.

For his achievements Dr. Sandage received the Nichols Cup for "outstanding service to advertising education" in 1963 from Alpha Delta Sigma, professional advertising fraternity, the Gold Medal Award for "distinguished service to advertising" in 1964 from *Printers' Ink*, the Advertising Federation of America, and the Advertising Association of the West, and a special award in 1966 from the American Association of Advertising Agencies for his contributions to advertising and advertising education.

Dr. Sandage has served as a director and vice president of the American Marketing Association. He also is a member of the American Economic Association, American Academy of Advertising, Association for Education in Journalism, American Association for Public Opinion Research, Alpha Delta Sigma, Delta Sigma Phi, professional business fraternity, Phi Beta Kappa, Kappa Tau Alpha, and Phi Kappa Phi.

He has written numerous magazine and journal articles and is the author or co-author of such books as *Advertising Theory and Practice* (now in its seventh edition), *Radio Advertising for Retailers, The Role of Advertising, The Promise of Advertising,* and *Readings in Advertising and Promotion Strategy.*

Dr. Sandage has also taught at Simpson College, University of Kansas, Miami University (Ohio), University of Cincinnati,

University of California, and the Harvard Graduate School of Business Administration. He has held executive positions with the U.S. Department of Commerce, Institute of Transit Advertising, and the Office of Price Administration. He also has served as a consultant to the Federal Communications Commission.

Dr. Sandage continues active as the president of the Farm Research Institute, a firm he founded in 1946 for continuous panel research of the Illinois and Indiana farm population, and as a consultant to various firms.

Born in Hatfield, Missouri, in 1902, he was married to the late Dorothy Briggs. They had one son, Allan, a renowned research astronomer with Mount Wilson and Mount Palomar observatories. He married Elizabeth Danner in 1971.

Dr. Sandage received his bachelor's and master's degrees and his doctorate degree in economics, all from the State University of Iowa.

Although his career is one of notable personal accomplishments, his students and associates are more likely to think of him as a man who has directed his energies primarily toward helping others realize their dreams and aspirations.

Contents

Frontiers of Advertising Theory and Research

Introduction

To the colleagues of Dr. Charles H. Sandage, a symposium in his honor seemed a fitting means to mark his retirement. What more appropriate tribute to a scholar could be devised than an occasion on which the intellectual questions to which he had long addressed himself might be further explored? The papers comprising this volume were presented at Allerton House, conference center of the University of Illinois, on May 23–24, 1968. They constitute not only a collective tribute to Dr. Sandage but also a substantial contribution to the literature of advertising and marketing.

The theme of the symposium—"The Frontiers of Advertising Theory and Research"—was chosen in recognition of Dr. Sandage's pioneering work in both of these aspects of the field and of the forward-looking spirit of his continuing endeavors. The range of material explored by the symposium reflects the scope of Professor Sandage's own scholarly concerns and achievements, which in the words of one participant, encompass advertising "as a science, a discipline, an art, and a way of life."

The papers presented at Allerton House logically fall into three broad categories: theoretical approaches to advertising as a social and economic institution; advertising research; and educational preparation for the teaching and practice of advertising. These represent the main currents in the writing, teaching, administration, and advocacy of C. H. Sandage.

As those acquainted with Dr. Sandage—as teacher, author, platform speaker, colleague, or fellow committee member—well know, one of his fundamental tenets is that advertising will take its place among the professions only after it has become socially responsible in all of its practices. The first two papers deal predominantly with ethics. The first is by Professor Otis A. Pease, author of the landmark volume *The Responsibilities of American Advertising* (Yale, 1958), and the second by Frank C. Hale of the Federal Trade Commission. These two and the one following, the comprehensive essay by Professor O. J. Firestone, distinguished Canadian economist, "An Economist Looks at Advertising," point up another vital concern of Dr. Sandage, that advertising be accorded its rightful role as a basic institution in contemporary society. Professor Firestone skillfully analyzes advertising's economic role, attributing to it functions that economic theorists—whether they are members of the classical, neo-classical, or welfare schools—have preferred to deny or ignore. Dr. Wendell R. Smith, former head of the Marketing Science Institute and now dean of the School of Business Administration, University of Massachusetts, cites trends to show that viable theories of marketing and advertising have recently emerged which afford new bases for systematic analysis and research. In discussing "Science and Advertising Theory," Dean Smith classifies advertising as practiced in the developed economies as a scientifically based discipline, thus documenting a view long held by the honoree of this symposium.

The six papers grouped under the heading "Frontiers of Advertising Research" focus attention on the area of advertising in which Dr. Sandage himself has been engaged most consistently.

The challenges laid down by the late Sherwood Dodge, president of the Advertising Research Foundation until his death a few days after the symposium ("Colonizing the Frontiers of Advertising Research"), serve as a keynote to the papers that follow as well as a valedictory to his own distinguished career. Mr. Dodge made a cogent assessment of the present state of advertising research, of which he was not particularly sanguine, and suggested the rigorous steps to be taken before it could hope to fulfill its potential. The next four papers, by assignment limited to narrower subject matter, deal with the "present state of the art," so to speak, in the application of behavioral science concepts and methodology ("software") and electronic technology ("hardware"), and predict what future research can be expected to yield for problems of management, measurement, and strategy.

Dr. Seymour Banks, media and programs research manager of the Leo Burnett Company, more "bullish" than the other speakers, sees breakthroughs for advertising experimentation and measurement in the "real-life situation" laboratories now provided by CATV and other television applications. A. Edward Miller, former president of the Alfred Politz Research Company, appraises the survey method, with which he has had so much experience, and recommends improved techniques in his paper ("Survey Approaches in Advertising"). In a parallel paper ("Psychological Approaches in Advertising Research"), Dr. Burleigh B. Gardner, president of Social Research, Inc., reports on progress and promise in applying behavioral concepts. He insists that the tests and techniques must be administered and interpreted by "professionals." Peter Langhoff, an engineer by training, who heads the American Research Bureau, presents his candid views on the utilization of computer technology for the solution of problems in the advertising business. He thinks the use of computers for bookkeeping functions only is a flagrant waste, and he excoriates agencies for letting the creative types eschew experimentation with computers. He does point out, however, areas where computers can be of immediate help—media buying and sales-movement recording, for example.

The demanding task of prognosticating future trends and achievements in advertising research was assigned to Dr. Leo Bogart, executive vice president of the Bureau of Advertising ("Where Does Advertising Research Go From Here?"). Like Sherwood Dodge, he points the way research must go to transcend its present parochial approach. He feels that the study of advertising institutions and of advertising as a communication process—two untapped areas that will yield valuable information—is so costly that it must find new sponsors—preferably not the "Establishment."

The third group of papers ("Frontiers of Advertising Education") was grouped with the "theory" papers in the symposium program. It seemed to the editor of this volume, however, that their importance accorded them a separate category. Dr. Sandage's persistent interest in the theory and practice of advertising education lends support to this view. It is on this subject, in fact, that he chose to make his own contribution to the symposium—an enunciation of his views, his philosophy of advertising education. As he builds his case for the ideal advertising curriculum, the reader is treated to the whole spectrum of his credo regarding the social and economic role of advertising as an institution. William A. Marsteller, founder and chairman of the successful agency bearing his name, friend of Dr. Sandage, and of advertising education, outlined his views as the featured banquet speaker of the symposium. As board member of the James Webb Young Fund, former educational committee chairman of the American Association of Advertising Agencies, and alumnus of the University of Illinois, he is well qualified to discuss the question. Last among the honoring papers is the report of John Crichton, president of the American Association of Advertising Agencies, of his recent industry-wide survey of the educational background of top agency executives. His analysis of his findings provides an objective base for his own views of "The Role of Advertising Education." He contrasts and compares his own education for advertising in the University of Missouri School of Journalism with present trends and reflects the views held by the leading practitioners.

HUGH W. SARGENT

I. FRONTIERS OF ADVERTISING THEORY

CHAPTER 1

Advertising, Its Ethics and Its Critics

by Otis A. Pease

Dr. Pease is professor and chairman of the Department of History, University of Washington. He formerly taught at the University of Texas and Stanford University. His published books include The Progressive Years, The Responsibilities of American Advertising, *and* Parkman's History.

I am not certain what you expect an historian to say to a gathering of advertising and marketing people. A scholar is always willing to believe that an audience familiar with his book is looking forward to hearing more on the same subject. At least fifteen years ago my good friend and former professor David Potter urged historians to make a serious examination of the institution of advertising. I am afraid that the example he set and I attempted to follow has been a lonely one. You honor me with your invitation to participate in a symposium to pay tribute to Professor Sandage, a distinguished fellow scholar who has been concerned throughout his career that advertising maintain a system of ethics worthy of a profession. Yet the study I published ten years ago did not view American advertising with complacency, and it is difficult for me to guess whether, all unconsciously, you asked me to address you in *spite* of some of the things I wrote then or *because* of them. And this uncertainty leads to the theme of my remarks.

For at least fifty years now, whenever they gather in convention or publish in symposia, advertising men have been accustomed to flagellating themselves over the presumed failure of

their social image and then, in curious and relentless alternation, they proceed to nurse their scarred egos. In what month
since 1920 has the editorial page of an advertising journal failed
to exhort the business to confess its misdeeds and renounce
sin? When have advertising men ever met together without
hearing from a critic? The more cutting his comments, the
better his audience has appeared to like them. If Schlesinger is
unavailable, Galbraith will do. (A generation ago it used to be
Stuart Chase or Rexford Tugwell.) Then, having writhed in
gratifying pain, having, as it were, rubbed salt on the cuts,
have they ever failed to find some other august outsider—often
a resident of the White House—to pour on the ointment?

If I say this with the assurance of a scholar who has studied
your history, I say this also with the astonishment of an historian whose own profession exhibits far less of an appetite for
masochism. Neither historians nor, I believe, economists, law-
yers, scientists, nor even professors of marketing have seemed
as concerned as advertising men over their professional failings,
the state of their ethics, or the remarks of their critics. Nor have
they apparently been as concerned to reassure themselves of the
validity and virtue of what they are doing. When a profession
is young and unestablished and craves respect, this behavior is
not hard to understand. In the 1960's advertising is neither
young nor unestablished, and it has won from society considerable respect for what it sets out to do. Yet it continues to
worry.

As an historian I want to explore a few of the continuing and
persistent forces that reveal themselves in this record of behavior.

There exists, of course, the disturbing possibility that advertising men have deserved to worry about themselves. A few
years ago Charlie Brown came to Lucy in great distress to seek
her help. While she sat behind her booth under that terrifying
sign which announces that the Psychiatrist is In, Charlie Brown
confessed his troubles. He said he felt inferior. People despised
him. He saw himself as unloved, unwanted. What was the matter? What was his problem?

Lucy had an answer. "Your problem, Charlie Brown, is not

that you *feel* inferior. Your problem is that you *are* inferior. 5¢ please."

To a considerable extent the outsider looking at advertising has echoed Lucy's diagnosis, often in the same spirit. More remarkably, the same diagnosis has been shared by many insiders who cared deeply about their work.

Now the question whether advertising was "inferior" was never capable of being objectively resolved, and was to that extent meaningless. But what historically was anything but meaningless—and what in fact constituted a major force in generating a degree of self-identity for men in advertising—was a significant effort to achieve three things: (1) a system of ethics; (2) a rationale for the profession and activity of advertising as a way of responding to critics and reducing opposition; and (3) a social role for advertising that transcended the basic function of merely serving the sellers of private goods and services. I wish to examine each of these three features for its relevance to the continuing problems of advertising: its self-image, its external image, and its critics.

A SYSTEM OF ETHICS

The growth of a system of ethics in the advertising business has a long and complex history, which it is not my intention to review here.[1] At its most visible this system was embodied in codes formulated voluntarily inside the advertising business and enforced largely from within, and in state or federal regulations based occasionally on advertising codes and enforced from without. Most of the internal codes took shape by the 1930's, and their character is amply suggested by the well-publicized Copy Code of the major advertising associations, adopted in the 1920's and still in existence forty years later. The code enumerated seven "practices that are unfair to the public and tend to discredit advertising."

1. False statements or misleading exaggerations.
2. Indirect misrepresentation of a product, or service, through distortion of details, either editorially or pictorially.
3. Statements or suggestions offensive to public decency.
4. Statements which tend to undermine an industry by attributing

to its products, generally, faults and weaknesses true only of a few.

5. Price claims that are misleading.
6. Pseudoscientific advertising, including claims insufficiently supported by accepted authority, or that distort the true meaning or application of a statement made by professional or scientific authority.
7. Testimonials which do not reflect the real choice of a competent witness.[2]

In addition to codes setting forth ethical precepts concerning advertisements, the industry, particularly under the authority of the Better Business Bureaus and other trade associations, also attempted to standardize approved practices in agency relations with clients and with media, including principles and methods of compensation.

External regulations generally reflected a body of ethical norms backed by laws governing federal agencies such as the Food and Drug Administration (briefly), and the Federal Communications Commission, or by state statutes such as those (found now in virtually every state in the Union) that are based on the Model Statute of 1911, first proposed by advertising men and given wide circulation by the advertising journal *Printers' Ink.* The statute declared that any person who placed before the public an advertisement "containing any assertion or statement of fact which is untrue, deceptive or misleading, shall be guilty of a misdemeanor."

Anyone who has examined in detail the history of the internal search for ethical standards would find it hard not to conclude that it arose not really from a desire to benefit the public or to safeguard the consumer (though these were often by-products) but rather from a desire to preserve the effectiveness of advertising. Bruce Barton stated it succinctly and authoritatively in 1935. No advertiser, he declared, should be permitted to act in such a way as to "poison the pond in which we all must fish."[3] (It was perfectly clear that what Barton had in mind was a concern not for the fish but for the fishermen.) Put more positively (as it usually was), the function of advertising codes and ethical systems was to preserve maximum credibility for advertising as a whole, consistent with its function as a weapon in marketing.

Many of the issues that generated support for certain portions of these codes seem distant and irrelevant today. There was, for example, considerable agitation in the 1920's over the use of testimonials. The more fastidious among the advertising men feared public revulsion against testimonials that had plainly been solicited and paid for. The concern of most advertising men diminished when it was discovered that the public regarded testimonials with noticeable tolerance and that testimonial advertising appeared to pay off. Then there was the continuing concern over advertising that "knocked the competitor." Not only did the codes denounce such practices, but also the Federal Trade Commission was vigilant to curb unduly competitive copy. Ironically, this kind of advertising could be regarded as possessing a fundamental advantage to the consumer. In 1928 the American Tobacco Company urged women who were concerned with their weight (and what women are not?) to "reach for a Lucky instead of a sweet." The ethics of the industry clearly condemned the use of this disparaging but undeniably accurate slogan, even as it prevented the candy manufacturers from retorting with equal accuracy that chocolate cigarettes would never harm the lungs or shorten lives. The ethical system that forbade "knocking the competitor" may or may not have served the consumer. The point is, it was designed fundamentally to serve the advertiser, and any other benefit was to be accounted a chance by-product.

It would not do to make too much of this. Advertising could not have survived without a system of ethics, for such a system was nothing less than a way of encouraging predictability in the behavior that governed relations among agencies, clients, media, and the institutions of marketing. There was no time when it, like any system, was not found in need of repair and even some re-structuring. Advertising men appeared to cling persistently to the notion that one obvious way to answer the critics of advertising was to repair and tighten its ethical codes. The critics of advertising, unfortunately, raised issues that the system of ethics, as we have seen, was not directly designed to solve.

A RATIONALE FOR THE PROFESSION

What did the advertising business do in response to its critics and in response to its own persistent concern for status and success? Again, we must condense a long and complex story.

The critics, of course, were a varied lot, and their criticism ranged widely. In less than a generation following the First World War, advertising swept across the land as a powerful revolutionary force. It overturned ancient and pervasive systems of value. Reacting against the ethos of the producer who believed in thrift and frugality, advertising countered with a doctrine of consumption. It is not surprising that advertisements would breed profound resistance, doubts, despair, and resentments. The most effective and persistent critics actually had no quarrel with the doctrine of consumption. They were themselves reformers, heirs to the Progressive tradition, and they favored political and social action that would strengthen capitalism by broadening its benefits. They believed in encouraging reason in human affairs and efficiency in the conduct of business and the market. These critics saw modern advertising as subversive of reform ideals even while it held out glowing promises of the Good Life. But though they did not object to greater consumption, they strongly objected to the particular social values that most advertising transmitted for the purpose of encouraging consumption. More than anything else, what they found deeply disturbing about advertising was a feature that lay at the core of modern marketing. That was its effort to shape consumer preferences to suit the needs of the competitive productive system rather than to assist consumers in translating their preferences rationally into a demand that producers would then satisfy. At least this is the way most of the critics—who were, I repeat, heirs to the political and social tradition of reform—interpreted the goals and the thrust of modern advertising. Their opposition went beyond merely stating a demand for factual accuracy and an end to misrepresentation. It offered a powerful practical challenge in the form of an organized, articulate consumer movement, an attempt to establish a united front among legislators, local retail organizations, professional groups like the American Medical Association, federal agencies like the Food and Drug Administration, and ultimately an appeal to the political power of the New Deal itself at a time when the Great Depression produced a general disenchantment with the nation's system of production and marketing.

Faced with a serious challenge to its role, the advertising industry displayed for the first time in its history a capacity to act as a single institution and to articulate something approaching a rationale for its behavior, the sort that would lead in time to greater professionalism in its work. It began to think seriously about the economic and social effects of what it was doing. (Among other things it discovered—after the event—that the doctrine of consumption possessed strong social merit during a depression.) It began to look for ways to convince consumers that despite the obvious faults of an institution dedicated to selling, its net benefit to society was on the whole positive. The advertising industry most commendably, I think, came to terms with itself and with its public in trying to make clear that it was not an institution of public service. It was a business, and it did not deserve to be judged adversely—as it was usually judged—either for failing to be a public service or for failing to rise above the limitations of the goods and services it was selling. An advertising firm, like a legal firm, could refuse a dubious client. Once it accepted a client, it was obliged to do its utmost for him. Except where the law required it, advertising was responsible not to the consumer but to the client.

As for the issue of "honesty" in the business of selling, the public had possibly been led by critics—and even on occasion by advertising men themselves—to expect too much. Critics insisted on drawing a sharp line between truth and falsity for acts of persuasion, and they insisted that such a line would lead consumers to develop the sort of rational behavior that alone permits a free market to survive. But this, said the advertising man, was an unreal picture of the social institution of marketing. The question of truth or falsity was real enough, but it was irrelevant in the way critics framed it, for the fundamental appeal of an advertisement lay not in its factual assertions but in the associations that it set up in the mind of the reader. There was no reasonably objective way of measuring or controlling this except to outlaw the appeal itself. Consumer preferences, finally, were never fixed and seldom pre-determined. They often remained obscure to the consumer himself. If advertising attempted to shape them, its action involved not a substitution of a non-rational for a rational response but rather the articulation of a response that was non-rational to begin with but that curiously could be seen as acquiring a degree of rationality in the very act of being embodied in the words and symbols of the advertisement.

By the time of the Second World War, then, I think we can say that the advertising industry had strengthened itself in consequence of the serious and not entirely unwarranted challenge to its social role. More to the point, it had gained strength as a profession by the serious and responsible studies it sponsored both of itself and of the entire institution of marketing. This was in part the consequence of the increasing attention that scholars in the largest universities were according the advertising and marketing process; it was at this time, for example, that Professor Neil Borden of the Harvard Graduate School of Business Administration completed his meticulous and searching study of the economic effects of advertising. The institution of advertising was also growing in effectiveness, and the reasons are not hard to state. In the years since 1939 the American consumer has made spectacular gains in discretionary purchasing power, which is clearly the lifeblood of advertising. No less important have been the wide advances since 1945 in marketing and consumer research. Most spectacular of all the forces for increased effectiveness of advertising has been the coming of television since 1950. It is perhaps unkind, though not inaccurate, to suggest, that while the critics had forced the advertising industry to respond to them, it was increasingly likely that the industry, possessing new weapons and a strengthened base of power, would ignore them.

Yet the critics persisted, and they continue to persist, and the advertising industry continues to worry about them, and in its worry betrays profound uneasiness about itself, its ultimate function, and its social role.

A SOCIAL ROLE FOR ADVERTISING

Could it really be that at bottom advertising lacks a social role as we customarily use the term? Here, possibly, the advertising man confronts his most serious dilemma.

What has the industry done to serve society as a whole and in the direct and easily visible ways we associate with the school or the church or the medical or legal profession? These institutions all possess a self-generating ethic of social utility based on a broad, almost universal, acceptance of their fundamental aims. The ready answer one hears from advertising men is that their transcendent social service is the stimulation of private consumption. Is this today a sufficiently compelling claim for a favorable judgment from society or for a favorable verdict from advertising men themselves? I do not profess to know, but in wondering about the continuing persistence of doubts and self-doubts about advertising, I will venture an uneasy observation.

Education, religion, medicine, law, and scholarship all appear to possess a kind of ultimate validity for American society. Their goals are perceived for the most part as good for all times and under all circumstances. Concerning the ultimate validity of advertising—the stimulation of private consumption—we are by no means as certain. Is it, for example, good for all times and under all circumstances? What about a period of high income but insufficient production, as in time of military action abroad? What about an occasion of grossly distorted national income? What about the social value of urging large numbers of Americans to desire perfectly legitimate goods and services that are utterly beyond their present capacity to acquire and in circumstances where a maldistribution of employment, education, and income makes it impossible for them to translate their desires into effective action? The great social ills of our time include poverty, misperceptions of race, legal and political injustices, a hopeless urban sprawl, the clumsiness of government, the pervasive ignorance and mistrust of public fiscal policy. The other major institutions—even the press and the broadcasting media—are conspicuously concerned with these issues. But what of the institution of advertising? By its very nature how can it concern itself with them? It may be the strength of advertising to remain the selling arm of individual business enterprise. Americans of the next generation, whose problems transcend the concerns of individual business enterprise and cry out for broad social solutions, may well withhold their ultimate approval of advertising until it can devise ways to act in concert on behalf of society itself, not merely fitfully, in response to individual clients or with the episodic caution of the National Advertising Council, but continuously and with an effort worthy of the terrible disorders and malfunctions that daily appear to mock our extraordinary talents to consume and possess.

Then at last, if that is what they want, advertising men may discover that they have entered the kingdom of saints.

NOTES

[1] For extended reading on this subject see C. H. Sandage and Vernon Fryburger (eds.), *The Role of Advertising* (Homewood, Ill.: Irwin, 1960), pp. 429–499; and Otis A. Pease, *The Responsibilities of American Advertising* (New Haven: Yale University Press, 1958), pp. 44–86, 115–166.

[2] Reproduced in *Printers' Ink*, May 26, 1932, p. 52.

[3] Quoted in *Printers' Ink*, Dec. 12, 1935, p. 17.

CHAPTER 2

Advertising and the Federal Trade Commission

by Frank C. Hale

Mr. Hale is director of the Bureau of Deceptive Practices, Federal Trade Commission, and a recipient of the Commission's Distinguished Service Award. Between 1963 and 1965 he served the State of Hawaii as Special Deputy Attorney General, consulting on antitrust and consumer protection. He has been chairman of the Federal Bar Association's Antitrust and Trade Regulation Committee and a member of the Administrative Conference of the United States, created by President Kennedy in 1961 for improving federal administrative agency procedures.

The more I have learned of Professor C. H. ("Sandy") Sandage, the more I can understand why you are paying tribute to him. Native of Missouri, educated in Iowa and Illinois, Phi Beta Kappa, high school teacher, business, marketing, and economics professor at college and university level, author, valued federal employee—these are but some of his accomplishments. And now after twenty years he is retiring as Head of the Department of Advertising at this great University of Illinois. How rich, how rewarding such a career!

We at the Federal Trade Commission do not pose as experts on what is good or effective advertising, especially not around people like Dr. Sandage. But because of the Federal Trade Commission's responsibilities, we have had considerable experience with advertising that is false, misleading, or deceptive. It is those responsibilities and the Commission's efforts to carry them out that I propose to discuss with you today.

I need not dwell on what advertising is or what its purposes are. I know there are many aspects of advertising in this country on which we in government and you in industry and education are fully agreed. For example, we all know most advertising serves a great purpose in stimulating production and encouraging competition for ever-improved goods and services for the American people. We are agreed it has played a vital part in creating the consumer demand that has made possible mass production and the consequent availability at reasonable prices of countless products. And we are well aware that advertising has encouraged Americans to know about and to strive for an even higher standard of living. The tremendous contribution that advertising has made to the nation's economic vitality is both conceded and applauded.

Some might then say that if advertising serves so great a purpose, why do we have the Federal Trade Commission? The answer requires a little history for prologue, history that does credit to the advertising industry.

ESTABLISHMENT OF THE FTC

Some 56 years ago a group of reputable advertisers promoted a Crusade for Truth in Advertising. These reputable members of the profession, including all segments, became fed up with the phony advertising that their unprincipled competitors were using. I'm sure you've seen the old ads and have been horrified that such copy could ever have been accepted. It was no wonder that committees of reputable advertisers were set up to try to halt it. They were motivated not only by a humane interest in protecting consumers, but also by their own interest in building greater public confidence in advertising. They realized that their advertising dollars were being devalued because of mounting public distrust of all advertising. Like the cat that walked on a hot stove and thereafter avoided all stoves, the consumer who was misled and deceived by one ad put precious little faith in any other.

The crusade was effective, and its momentum continued. Although pressure could be brought to improve the credibility of local ads, the problem of nationwide advertising remained.

Thus, in 1913, wholehearted bipartisan support was given to a proposal before Congress that an interstate trade commission be created to halt unfair methods of business competition in interstate commerce. To this idea President Woodrow Wilson added his own very important blessing. The result was the creation in 1914 of the Federal Trade Commission. Here was an instrument of government sired and fashioned by your predecessors. It was not forced down from on high. It was requested by them from their government to help them in their crusade for truth in advertising. It was a grass-roots victory.

In the words of President Wilson, the Commission would serve as "an indispensable instrument of information and publicity, as a clearing house for the facts by which the public mind and the managers of great business undertakings shall be guided, and as an instrumentality for doing justice to business where the processes of the courts or the natural forces of correction outside the courts are inadequate to adjust the remedy to the wrong in a way that will meet the equities and circumstances of the case."

The Commission's adversary actions, its formal complaints and orders in both fields—restraint of trade, and deceptive practices—have occasioned most of the news coverage given our agency. For this reason the idea has been widespread that the Commission conducts a policing operation. This is true only for certain laws—the Wool, Fur, and Textile Labeling Acts and the Flammable Fabrics Act. But the Commission's basic responsibilities arise from enforcement of four sections of the Clayton Act, including Section 2, as amended by the Robinson-Patman Act, and enforcement of the Federal Trade Commission Act. Of course, we now also have some very important functions to perform under the Federal Cigarette Labeling and Advertising Act, and the Fair Packaging and Labeling Act.

But to get back more particularly to the FTC Act. The idea behind it was to prevent the development of monopolistic empires that could be built up by unfair methods of competition. Later, in 1938, the Act was broadened to prohibit deceptive business practices regardless of their competitive effect.

In its basic purposes, the Commission was intended to serve

business not simply as a regulator but as a guide capable of identifying and halting unfair and deceptive business practices.

The Commission's casework and its guides might well be compared to the lights and buoys that mark a river's channel. It is a lot easier and cheaper to guide advertisers away from the shoals of deception than to clean up the wreckage. Yet there are some few, who, oblivious of the public interest, would set their course across the shoals of the law in seeking a short-cut to the quick dollar. To them, the marking of a safe channel represents unwarranted government interference, particularly if the warning light shines on their own operations.

We do not believe that the great reputable segment of the advertising industry has looked upon the Commission's guidance role as representing "unwarranted government interference." On the contrary, I am sure you will agree that it has served to reduce, if not eliminate, the need for sterner restrictions on business freedom.

In more than 53 years of defining the limits of legality by which proper advertising can be measured, the Commission has eliminated a great deal of uncertainty. For this, I am certain all reputable advertisers are grateful; for nothing is more frustrating to businessmen than to try to stay within a law whose edges cannot be defined exactly, while less scrupulous competitors take full advantage of the grey areas across the borderline.

Thus, in creating the Commission, Congress recognized that the guidance of an administrative agency was needed to implement the intent of a law that had to be stated in broad language. It would have been impossible back in 1914—or later at the time of the 1938 amendments to the FTC Act, and even now—to frame definitions to embrace all unfair practices that existed or could be invented. Therefore the law expressed the Congressional intent to halt "unfair methods of competition and unfair or deceptive acts or practices," and the FTC is the agency the Congress created and empowered to illuminate and give force to that intent in an expanding and ever-changing economy.

I have given this much background simply to emphasize that

the Commission's role and purpose have always been one of guidance. It has never been and never will be a Gestapo. For this we can all be grateful.

SHIFT IN FTC POLICY

There may be some who are not fully aware of the greater emphasis the Commission has been giving in recent years to the guidance principle. This is in marked contrast to the policy dominant during the earlier and greater period of its history —the bringing of formal actions against individual companies whenever investigation indicated the law was being violated. Formal action was undertaken in expectation that application of the trade laws would be clarified and that others engaged in the same or similar illegalities would mend their ways lest they, too, be faced with a lawsuit. This policy of suing as many firms as FTC manpower could manage did indeed build up a formidable body of case law.

Former Commissions were able to point with pride to the resulting statistics of complaints and orders. Numbers were hailed as the measure of the FTC's competence. This is not to say that the Commission did not provide industry-wide guidance to those who sought it, but the dominant idea was to sue, and, by publicizing each case at every stage in its prosecution, to educate business and the public as to what the Commission considered unfair or deceptive—what advertising was deemed false and misleading.

The trouble with that technique was that too often one firm was made to suffer when it was not the only sinner, and those who were not caught kept right on sinning. Moreover the predators were well aware that the FTC was so overloaded with work involved in the case-by-case approach that their chances of getting caught were slim indeed. Even if they were caught, the work overload made for delay, and delay could be made profitable. In short, the FTC's efforts became not a drop in a bucket but a drop in a barrel.

Clearly, a new approach to achieve the Commission's purpose had to be found and developed. And it has been.

During the past six years, the Commission has, with ever-increasing effectiveness, endeavored to provide the tools wherewith the reputable and overwhelming majority of American businessmen can help keep their own house clean, and this includes their advertising.

What the Commission could never hope to do by itself if it pursued only the case-by-case approach, it now is doing by giving form, direction, and unity to the willingness—the eagerness—of most businessmen to rid their industries of the predatory practices and deceptive advertising of the few. Competitive pressures had forced many to "fight fire with fire," and they welcomed the Commission's invitation to quit the fire-fighting simultaneously. Even the few die-hard violators realized they would become conspicuous targets for formal Commission action. So, the desire, the willingness of the great majority of businessmen, advertisers, to abide by the law and to do so with confidence that their competitors would do likewise, has enabled the Commission to concentrate on the comparatively few willful violators.

This approach to law enforcement has not been without its problems. It has required more patience, more groundwork, and better judgment than taking pot shots at every target that has shown itself or been reported to us. And we do get a lot of "reports" from consumers and competitors alike. Our first concern in dealing with these reports is to consider whether there is a probable violation and to make a thorough enough investigation to resolve the question. Then we must consider whether it is an isolated problem, or regional or industry-wide. How broad should the recommended corrective action be? Would the public interest be protected by an assurance from the respondent that he will stop the illegal practice, or is formal action required? Does the violation stem from confusion as to the law's exact requirements? Could the difficulty be countered better by issuance of an industry guide or a trade regulation rule? Which of all the possibilities would ensure the quickest, the surest, and the most economical protection for the public and for the law-abiding advertiser? In short, each alleged law violation is analyzed to learn its extent and to consider how best to cope with it in terms of speed, fairness, and protection of the public interest. And if results can be achieved without fanfare, so much the better. The law is enforced without use of a trumpet or a smear brush.

COOPERATIVE VENTURES

A few years ago the Commission instituted still another procedure in its efforts to work and cooperate with industry. It will, if at all possible, render advisory opinions on the legality of proposed courses of action—proposed advertising copy, for example—to those who seek them.

The Commission's new approach to its responsibilities also includes a much closer working relationship with state and local authorities. In setting up an office for Federal-State Cooperation, the Commission has established closer communications with all 50 states. Thus it is often able to detect law violations before they can assume interstate proportions. Many of the complaints from consumers that are of a local nature and, therefore, not within our jurisdiction, are now being forwarded to state authorities. A number of states have enacted effective consumer protection laws and have established active programs. We believe that as this liaison becomes increasingly effective, it will go far toward halting chicanery that has been dodging from state to state.

With this background on the Federal Trade Commission of the present, I would add a further thought. I understand indirectly that some in the advertising business, while agreeing that the policies of the present Federal Trade Commission make good sense, have voiced the apprehension that, in the years ahead, future Commissions may reverse the field and go back to the old ways. As in the case of any Bureau Director, or anyone else at the staff level, my remarks today do not necessarily represent the views of the Commission, but I do think none will disagree that such a return is possible. But I also think it is most unlikely. To go back to the old numbers game instead of continuing to encourage self-discipline simply would not square with the problem.

The Commission will never be big enough to enforce the laws entrusted to it without a tremendous assist from reputable and farsighted businessmen, from those like you in the advertising field—be it as advertisers, agencies, or educators—who are participating in this symposium in honor of one who has contributed so much to the success and increasingly high order of advertising.

A CHALLENGE TO EDUCATORS

What I have said thus far is pretty much in the vein you might have expected, a description of the basic purposes of the Federal Trade Commission and how it is pursuing these purposes. But now there is a request I would make of you. This request is not made lightly. It warrants your most serious consideration. I ask you to examine your teaching or your practice of advertising to determine whether sufficient emphasis has been placed on the importance of honesty. Just plain honesty.

To a sophisticated audience, emphasizing the importance of honesty might seem naïve. Perhaps it is. But I believe that in our preoccupation with the techniques and intricacies of any profession, in this case advertising, we are likely to ride too lightly over basic morality. Presentation becomes more important than substance. How to milk an idea for profit supersedes the merit of the idea. And truth might become a problem, or even an irritant. Thus do we become so enmeshed in skill, in competence, in style, in daring, and in our own egos that we forget that truth and fairness are even more important.

Let us suppose I were addressing a different audience, an audience of young men and women out to make a buck in the glamorous profession of advertising. Would they pay any attention to the economic and moral need that led to the Commission's creation? Would they put much credence in the Commission's reliance on self-policing? Or would they listen most carefully to statements concerning our limited capacity? Would their ears be alert to the nuisance potential of the Commission, or to its usefulness in guiding them in the preparation of lawful advertising, even at the risk of displeasing a future client? I won't attempt to answer these questions. I simply offer them to you.

Of one thing I am sure. Anything I might say about the Federal Trade Commission and its purposes would be discredited by the prematurely sophisticated as being urged in self-interest. To them, any civil servant would, of course, argue for the necessity of the agency that has him on the payroll. Sure, he would quote what Woodrow Wilson said in 1913, fifty-five years ago, about the Commission being a clearing house for the facts by which the public mind and the managers of great business undertakings shall be guided. To them, he could also be expected to say that his agency was doing a magnificent job worth even more of the taxpayers' dollars. So, the question becomes one of how to make them believe that the Federal Trade Commission was a great concept in gaining compliance with the law.

This is where you come in.

University professors, and associate professors and instructors, too, command the respect of both undergraduate and graduate students. Students also respect those who have proved their competence in the outside world of competition. To both they will listen with attention and respect. They are avid to learn the savvy of success. Perhaps some students are concerned with the morality of the marketplace, but the hard drivers are more concerned with the "how" than the "why" of conquering the world of advertising.

I suggest that educators and businessmen would do well to lay more stress on the need to tell the truth in advertising. They should do this not only because government counts heavily on self-policing to ensure compliance with the law, but also because honest dealing and honest advertising build reputability. A deserved reputation for reputability is worth all the tricks in the advertising bag.

Actually, the trade laws both command and reinforce honesty and fairness. These laws simply clarify and give force to what we in a free society believe is best for our economic well-being. Whether they will be obeyed depends on whether we deserve our heritage. And the time has come when such an elemental decision has become terribly important.

CHAPTER 3

An Economist Looks at Advertising

by O. J. Firestone

Dr. Firestone is professor of economics and vice dean of the Faculty of Social Sciences, University of Ottawa. He has served the Canadian government for many years as an economic advisor and research director, and has represented Canada at a number of international conferences. His published books include The Economic Implications of Advertising, Broadcast Advertising in Canada, Past and Future Growth, Problems of Economic Growth, *and* Industry and Education, A Century of Canadian Development.

It is a great privilege indeed for a Canadian to be invited to join so many distinguished American scholars and enlightened practitioners of the art of advertising to pay tribute to Professor C. H. Sandage, the retiring Head of the Department of Advertising of the University of Illinois, for his creative and devoted contributions to the theory and research of advertising. Today, I welcome this opportunity to say to Professor Sandage that his great achievements have not only contributed materially to professionalism in the advertising field, but they have also given academicians in the United States and in other countries a new orientation in their search for truth in a somewhat neglected and much maligned field of economic endeavour.

Your programme committee has given me a broad assignment under the heading "An Economist Looks at Advertising." I shall limit my comments to a few specialized aspects and

I shall present these in a framework of the effects of advertising, both positive and negative, on economic growth, economic development, and economic progress.

ABUNDANCE VERSUS WASTE

Professor Sandage describes advertising as the "institution of abundance."[1] Other economists speak of advertising with scorn, describing it, in total or in large part, as social waste. One of the leaders in the latter group is Professor John Kenneth Galbraith. Let me elaborate.

Professor Sandage says:

> The need for communication with consumers is great. Equally great is the need to stimulate and stretch the wants of consumers, both for private and public goods and services. It is in this realm that advertising, the institution of abundance, is of paramount importance.[2]

Professor Galbraith says: "For advertising men it has long been a sore point that economists dismissed them as so much social waste."[3]

Some critics may say that both Professor Sandage and Professor Galbraith are making too sweeping claims either in praising the virtues or in stressing the disutilities of advertising.

Professor Sandage belongs to a minority of professional economists who emphasize the need to examine the full contribution of advertising to the effective working of the economic system on the basis of factual evidence, both quantitative and qualitative, economic and non-economic, and a theoretical examination of the basic issues involved. There is merit in this approach, and I shall come back to Professor Sandage's reference to the contribution that advertising makes to abundance later on.

Professor Galbraith finds himself in an awkward position. He considers it fun to disagree with the economic fraternity and he enjoys making observations with tongue in cheek. But in this matter of criticizing advertising, Galbraith finds himself agreeing with the majority of professional opinions, and this includes many leading economists in the United States, the

United Kingdom and Canada, such as Kenneth Boulding,[4] Richard Caves,[5] Nicholas Kaldor,[6] and Harry Johnson.[7]

Professor Galbraith resolves this dilemma by going further than most of his colleagues. He does this by saying that not only does advertising lead to a misallocation of resources, but it is downright immoral, for it relies frequently on "palpable fantasy" rather than on "circumstantial evidence,"[8] and it contributes to "organized public bamboozlement." This state of affairs is looked at increasingly by the "intellectual community . . . with disdain" and it "deplores it as intellectually corrupt."[9]

Optimum Utilization and Consumer Sovereignty

Let us look at the wastefulness argument further. There are two basic aspects to it.

One is that it interferes with the objective of achieving optimum utilization of the factors of production on a sustained and sustainable basis, thereby contributing to a misallocation of resources. Examples include the claim that large advertising expenditures create artificial, unwarranted, and costly product differentiation or that they keep out new entrants to an industry in which the working of free market forces is tampered with by the operating policies of a few dominant oligopolists.

The other is that it interferes with the principle of consumer sovereignty. Consumers are assumed to be knowledgeable people who are interested in obtaining the maximum benefits from their spending. To the extent that advertising sways consumers to spend differently from what *they* consider to be in their best interest, it distorts "true" consumer preferences.[10]

Freedom of consumer choice, so the argument goes, becomes a hollow concept. As the power of persuasion grows, with large advertisers using mass media, the real decision-making process is being transferred from the "timid" consumer to "big" business. Consumer demand, instead of being individually initiated, becomes industry-managed, a group decision-making process which Galbraith describes as the "techno-structure."[11]

In essence, these two main objections revolve around the

questions: (1) whether and to what extent advertising affects adversely continuing economic growth, which involves the full utilization of expanding productive capacity, and (2) whether and to what extent advertising affects consumer decisions, both in specific as well as in aggregate terms.

These two subjects, which are interrelated, are discussed further on. Before proceeding, a more fundamental point needs to be considered: whether the present academic debate is not leading the profession into a blind alley.

Changing Concepts of Society

The criterion of wastefulness in the days when scarcity of resources was a major consideration had a most persuasive effect on the development of certain aspects of economic theory. Human wants have remained infinite, and economic capacity to meet these wants has remained limited. But in this age of the affluent society the question arises: Has the concept of scarcity the same meaning as it had in earlier periods when human progress was largely based on the survival of the fittest, and when social justice was a moral, philosophical, or religious concept, and was not as widely accepted as an economic concept, as is the case in many of the developed countries of the world at the present time?

In an ideal state of economic affairs, all waste could presumably be eliminated. But in real life some waste appears to be unavoidable either because people do not know that what they do involves some social waste, or if they do know, because they want to behave that way, and society gives them the freedom to do so.

Why do many well-to-do North American consumers change their cars every year even though they could continue to use their vehicles without much trouble for another year or two? Why do North American consumers insist on choosing their cars from a variety of over one hundred new models, when, say, a dozen models could meet most of their needs?

The European car manufacturer considers North American car-buying habits extravagant. And so does the European consumer. But the North American consumer does not think of it as waste but as a way of life. And the North American manufacturer is more than ready to oblige, and in fact fosters such consumer attitudes with all the means of persuasion at his disposal, because it is good business to do so.

The more affluent society becomes, the more waste it can afford. It can afford it for two reasons: First, because waste notwithstanding, output expands and with it increase the benefits that flow from it to society as a whole.[12] Second, because the price that society would have to pay to avoid or reduce some of the waste is greater than the community is prepared to pay.

There is little doubt that costs per car are higher in the United States and in Canada where manufacturers produce over one hundred models each year, than if they were to produce only about a dozen models. But the North American public appears to prefer the greater choice at higher prices per automobile to a more limited choice at lower prices, brought about either by government control or by industry agreements.

This is not to suggest that even the most affluent society in the world can afford "undue" waste. In the United States there are large unused, underutilized, and misused resources which, if more effectively employed, could contribute to a material reduction in economic and social distress. For improvements notwithstanding, poverty is still widespread in the United States. Somewhere close to one-fifth of the population live below subsistence standards and lack adequate economic opportunities to better themselves. A somewhat similar situation also prevails in Canada.[13]

If reduction of waste in the private and public sectors could lead to increasing output and more equitable distribution of income, it then becomes a primary task of the economist to show where, what, and how. But in his zeal to serve the social good, the economist must be aware of the need to blend the requirements of economic theory with the realities of individual preferences, remembering that the latter encompass also political, cultural, psychological, and social aspirations.

DYNAMICS OF ADVERTISING

Let us now come back to Professor Sandage's reference to advertising as "an institution of abundance." Two aspects are particularly noteworthy.

First, by singling out advertising as a means of aiding the pursuit of the objective of "abundance," Professor Sandage reminds us that we are living in an age of great technological advances. The latter make substantial expansion of wealth-creating capacity possible, if—and this applies particularly to the developed countries—people and their leaders have the will and are prepared to exert the effort to make effective use of the nation's growing productive potential. For abundance is the antidote to scarcity. The best way to defeat scarcity is to expand both the country's potential *and* actual Gross National Product, and distribute the latter in a manner that maximizes the benefits of such growth among the largest number realizable.[14]

Second, by using the phrase in the context of stimulating and stretching "the wants of consumers, both for private and public goods and services," Professor Sandage stresses the dynamic aspects of the role of advertising. For by expanding consumer wants, presumably along constructive lines,[15] society faces a new challenge: how to meet such growing and increasingly diversified consumer demands. Fortunately, the productive capacity of the economy is growing and with it the managerial, technical, and administrative skill and policy know-how which make it possible to translate expanding consumer wants into effective consumer demand, thus increasing the nation's output. This implies that advertising may be a factor of some significance in the economic growth process.

The flow of academic literature on economic growth has been voluminous, particularly in the last decade. But very little has been written about advertising and economic growth. Professor Sandage's statement implies that there is need to consider the subject further. Before dealing with it, a brief comment about concepts used may be helpful.

Economic Growth, Economic Development, and Economic Progress

Three terms are involved: economic growth, economic development, and economic progress. Some economists use these phrases interchangeably to describe the same or similar processes of economic expansion, while others advance three distinct and different concepts of social betterment. While the role of advertising in the growth process of modern nations is being dealt with in this paper more generally than a study in depth would permit, it may be useful to set out briefly the three definitions.

Economic growth takes place when a nation's output expands. It is usually measured in terms of an increase in the Gross National Product in real terms. Such economic growth may take place because the factors of production, land, labour, and capital, are expanding, and sufficient demand for the resulting goods and services is engendered to warrant an increase in the nation's output.

Economic growth can take place without productivity rising—that is, a unit of output being produced with a lesser input—without significant technological advances and without changes in the industrial and social structure. For if the factors of production are expanding, society is capable of creating a greater output of goods and services if demand for these also expands. But most nations are not satisfied with this type of economic growth. They aim also at continuously increasing productivity and they endeavour to achieve this objective through the adoption of technological advances, the application of entrepreneurial initiative, the accumulation and effective use of physical capital and human resources, changes in industrial structure, and the build-up of social investment, as well as the pursuit of appropriate economic policies conducive to economic advancement. When economic growth takes this form it is usually described as *economic development* and is measured in terms of changes in Gross National Product in real terms per person working, or in terms of output produced per man-hour.

When economic development occurs, economic growth also takes place. But the reverse is not necessarily the case. When economic growth occurs without economic development, little or no *economic progress* may be made, if economic progress is defined as an increase in the share of the nation's output available to each citizen. In this sense, economic progress can be measured in terms of changes in Gross National Product in real terms per capita.

For economic progress to take place, individual welfare has to increase, if not for all, for the majority of the population. Hence, measurement of economic progress also involves an assessment of changes in income distribution. Variations in income distribution may be the result of market forces and individual initiative, or of fiscal policies affecting income distribution, including a progressive income tax system and a broadly based social security and primary industry support programme.[16]

Kenneth Boulding is one of the economists who considers economic progress and economic development as two sides of the same coin and to him the terms are synonymous. Says Boulding:

> Economic progress is concerned solely with means, not with ends. It enables us to get what we want more easily than before, but it says nothing about the propriety of what we want. If we want the wrong things, then economic progress may enable us to damn ourselves all the more quickly. . . . Indeed, economic progress makes a critique of wants all the more necessary, for the better we are able to satisfy our wants the more important it is that our wants should be "good" wants.[17]

This reasoning, according to Boulding, applies with equal force to the manner in which economic progress affects the wants of individuals and of society as a whole.

The essence of the Boulding thesis is that economic progress is concerned not only with the ability of a person or of a nation to satisfy more effectively an expanding array of diverse wants, but also with the changing character of such wants. This distinction achieves particular meaning in conjunction with the claim that modern advertising efforts have been increasingly used to distort the consumer pattern.

This criticism revolves fundamentally around the premise that advertising encourages people to meet their material wants and to neglect non-material wants which are part of a fuller way of life. Professor Galbraith has expanded this criticism by saying that advertising has been a major factor in increasing private consumption at the expense of public consumption. As a result, economic growth in many developed countries, but particularly in the United States, has been unbalanced and based on a biased sense of values.[18]

Some economists do not agree with Galbraith that advertising may have much to do with social imbalance. Their answer given to Galbraith that "the full thrust of advertising, along with other forces, is to emphasize private consumption of goods and services at the expense of public consumption in the form of schools, education, better public buildings, wars on poverty, more social research, and so on" is: "This imbalance in spending creates public loss in that more gain in the quality of life would be derived from using resources this way rather than in expanded private consumption. Though such an imbalance exists, it is doubtful that it is strongly associated with advertising."[19]

Advertising and Economic Growth

Advertising can be said to contribute to economic growth if it aids the expansion of productive capacity and/or the demand for goods and services in sufficient volume to absorb fully or almost fully[20] the total output which the nation's growing resources are capable of producing. To put this statement in question form: Does advertising contribute to raising potential Gross National Product? Does advertising contribute to increasing actual Gross National Product?

Here are some of the ways in which advertising may contribute to raising *potential* Gross National Product:[21]

1. Advertising may contribute to increasing the size of the labour force, e.g., by informing married women of remunerative job opportunities or by persuading potential emigrants

of working age to seek their good fortune in another country.

2. Advertising may contribute to an improvement in the quality of the labour force and hence its productive potential, e.g., by providing information about educational and training opportunities.[22]

3. Advertising may contribute to expanding capital stock and changes in its composition, e.g., when industrial advertising encourages businessmen to buy new machinery and equipment.

4. Advertising may encourage firms to proceed with plant expansion or modernization to bring new or improved products on the market, e.g., when pilot studies or other investigations indicate that with appropriate promotional efforts an adequate sales volume can be attained to ensure the viability of the project.

Advertising may also aid in raising *actual* Gross National Product. These contributions may be related to Gross National Product or its equivalent, the Gross National Expenditure and its major components. Here are a few examples.

1. Advertising involves human efforts and it results in economic activity. People work in advertising, either directly or as suppliers of goods and services. They earn incomes or they make profits, and thus they contribute directly to Gross National Product. As more people are employed in the advertising industry and in related fields, and as their contributions to output and earnings rise, they increase actual Gross National Product.

2. Advertising assists some businessmen to make investment decisions. They look for increased productivity and expanded market shares. If they can be convinced that advertising will yield them a market for a new or improved product so that they can benefit from economies of scale, they are likely to proceed with plant expansion or improvement programmes. The resulting flow of capital spending represents one of the major dynamic variables in the economic growth process.

3. Advertising is being used increasingly by governments and

other public authorities to fulfil their functions more effectively. To the extent that this makes for more efficient
government and better communications between those who
govern and those who are governed, the way to economic
expansion is smoothed.

4. Advertising is used to some extent to promote exports and
imports of goods and services. Thus it affects the balance
of payments and the flow of net foreign investment. The
bulk of international trade however, like the bulk of business capital spending and government expenditures, is un-
affected by it. A variety of manufactured goods, particularly
consumer articles, and some foodstuffs, do depend on
advertising for their sale, including, for example, imports
of cameras and toys, coffee and tea, and exports of North
American-type cars and canned salmon.

To the extent that advertising facilitates exports of goods
and services, it contributes either directly to economic
growth through the additional employment and income
created in the export industry, or indirectly through the
multiplier effect and the acceleration principle.

At first glance, to the extent that advertising contributes
to an increase of the volume of imports, it detracts from
economic growth, for an additional inflow of goods and
services means a contribution to the economic growth of
the country of origin and not the country of destination.
But this is an oversimplification of the balancing effect of
international trade for the latter presumably brings economic benefits to all participating nations as the result of
increasing international division of labour. There is the
further point that balance of payment considerations require that over the longer term countries wishing to export
must also be prepared to import.

5. Advertising is employed more frequently to promote the
sale of consumer goods and services than it is used to affect
the flow of any other major components of Gross National
Expenditure. That advertising can influence the purchasing
decisions of millions of individuals is well established.
Whether it can also have a significant impact on consumer

spending in aggregate is a controversial subject. I shall come back to it later on.

Advertising and Economic Development

Economic development occurs when Gross National Product in real terms per person working or output produced per man-hour rises. This improvement in economic performance is commonly referred to as a productivity increase. Thus the question arises: If advertising makes a contribution to economic development, how does it affect individual and national productivity?

Productivity may be raised through increasing the performance capability of labour and management, improving the organization of the production and distribution process, changing the economic structure, and expanding investment in durable physical assets.

In some of these areas advertising plays only a minor role. But in one its contribution is more significant—its potential effect on the level and composition of business capital spending. In this respect its main influence stems from its effect on business decisions to introduce innovations, and to expand and modernize production and distribution facilities in order to serve expanding, and in many instances more competitive, markets.

As explained by Schumpeter, innovations involve "any 'doing things differently' in the realm of economic life."[23] The innovations most affected by advertising are new or improved products. For in modern times advertising has become an essential part of the selling and promotional efforts required to facilitate the marketing of new articles to consumers and to obtain public acceptance for them.

The introduction of new products in many instances involves substantial investment outlays. Businessmen, as a rule, are willing to proceed with such capital expenditures only if they are confident that a sufficient volume of sales can be achieved to ensure an adequate return on the investment allowing for the risk and the cost of money involved.

The entrepreneur "will endeavour to obtain acceptance of the new products by whatever promotional means he believes will serve this purpose, and this as a rule may include a carefully planned advertising program. To achieve consumer acceptance, he will aim at product differentiation by building up a brand-name item. He will endeavour to create in the minds of the consumers a confidence factor in the quality, usefulness and serviceability of the product, and he will attempt to achieve continuity in consumers' acceptance of this product."[24]

But it is not only new or improved products that may require large investment expenditures. Entrepreneurs also endeavour to expand markets for "old" products through large promotional efforts, including advertising, and if they succeed, they may require additional production capacity to serve expanding markets.

Having built up large markets for a differentiated product, businessmen often find competitors moving in on them. In order to retain their market share, they may find it necessary to improve either the product or its presentation, e.g., packaging, its marketing, e.g., by offering premiums, its serviceability, e.g., by extending warranty, its price, e.g., by underselling their competitors, a policy made possible by a reduction in the profit margin or an increase in productivity, or a combination of the two.

Raising productivity, in turn, depends to a significant extent on the size of the market. Thus the retention or expansion of market shares with the aid of effective advertising efforts becomes an essential objective of management policy in many consumer-oriented industries.

Introducing innovations and catering to expanded markets involve capital expenditures which have increasingly required larger and larger amounts of investment funds, not only because the costs of capital goods have risen more rapidly than the costs of most other goods and services, but also because of the growing complexity of technology and the increasing sophistication incorporated into new consumer goods.

The link between advertising and economic development may be direct. For example, advertising contributes to the expansion of sales of goods produced by high-productivity industries, and thus to a shift in the industrial structure of the economy. Another example would be the reduction of distribution costs through improved marketing or promotional techniques.

Even more numerous appear to be the indirect links between advertising and economic development. These cover the whole range of influences that lead to increasing investment, particularly that portion contributing to productivity improvements.

For investment to take place, savings are required. If, as some claim, advertising persuades consumers to spend more in aggregate terms than they would be prepared to do without advertising, savings are diminished. A reduction of domestic savings in turn will affect investment unless the reduction in domestic saving is made up by drawing on savings from abroad leading to net foreign investment.

To the extent that advertising can influence the national savings rate in a downward direction, it would affect the ability of the economy to increase and update its productive capacity, at least that part financed from domestic sources. In this case, the question arises: Does advertising under certain circumstances hinder economic development, or slow down its rate of advance?

The answer to this question is a qualified "yes," though admittedly there are situations in which advertising contributes to an increase of savings rather than to their reduction. Without trying to deal with the subject exhaustively, two situations may be noted in which advertising may affect economic development adversely.

Anti-Development Aspects of Advertising

Advertising may assist large business firms to interfere with the working of free market forces and the effective operation of the competitive system. According to the "power of the purse" argument,[25] advertising may assume such a role in the competitive system that it becomes a barrier to entry of new firms in industries where large promotional expenditures are a prerequisite of successful business operations.

This argument was presented by the former U.S. Assistant Attorney General, Donald F. Turner, in these terms:

> When heavy advertising and other promotional expenditures create durable preferences going beyond the relative superiority of the product, resistant to anything but major countervailing promotional campaigns, we may well question whether the price has not become too high. If heavy advertising expenditures thus serve to raise the barriers to entry, the adverse competitive consequences are important not only because new firms are kept out, but also because frequently it is the prospect of new entry which serves as a major competitive restraint upon the actions of existing firms. . . . entry will be made more difficult as a result of the barriers created through extensive advertising.[26]

Some economists counter the Turner argument by saying that the entry of new firms into an industry is affected by many factors, of which advertising may be one, and in most instances not a particularly important one. Hence, they claim that proper assessment of the conditions of entry requires an evaluation of *all* the factors bearing on entry, and that by singling out advertising as the main or a major culprit, the critics are oversimplifying a complex problem.[27]

The other anti-development feature of advertising arises only if the claim that advertising can contribute to raising aggregate consumer spending in relation to aggregate income is valid. For in that case, a reduction of personal savings may affect the capacity of the economy to finance a rise in investment in the volume required to achieve sustained and increasingly diversified economic expansion.

Assuming for the moment that advertising under certain circumstances may contribute to an increase in aggregate consumer spending—the arguments for and against this supposition are presented later under the heading "Advertising and Economic Progress"—it would thus be a factor in altering the ratio of personal savings to personal disposable income.

The argument that advertising contributes to an increase in aggregate consumer spending and a reduction in aggregate personal savings usually refers to a situation as a point in time or during a comparatively short accounting or survey period, say a quarter or a year. The question arises whether this is not an oversimplification of the spending and saving process if the latter is considered in the context of a longer time period.

Advertising may affect the volume of individual savings directly. For example, people may increase their savings in response to a government savings-bond drive. Or they may heed the appeals of financial institutions, e.g., to open savings accounts with a bank, or to buy life insurance. Then there are other types of savings which are indirectly affected by advertising, and they occur following periods of dissavings.

The economies of North America rely increasingly on consumer buying on credit. A good deal of this credit buying leads to dissavings, defined as a state of affairs where families spend more than they earn. Following Professor Katona, three different types of dissavings may be identified:

1. Inability to meet necessary expenditures out of income. An example would be emergency expenditures, e.g., to pay for heavy costs of illness.
2. Unwillingness to keep *usual* expenditures within the level of income earned. An example would include people keeping up their spending notwithstanding a decline in income, e.g., temporary unemployment.
3. Unwillingness to keep unusual expenditures within the level of income earned. Examples would include the purchase of a house, major consumer durable goods, or luxury items or comfort services, e.g., an extended holiday trip.[28]

Dissavings of categories (1) and (2) are more likely to occur among lower-income groups and they may not be affected significantly by advertising. Dissavings of category (3) are more likely to occur among people in middle- and higher-income brackets. In these cases advertising may have a significant effect on the purchases of consumer goods and services and these, particularly if they involve larger expenditures, may lead to dissavings.

Dissavings will occur when people have some financial strength to back up their borrowing capacity. "They must have assets to sell, previous savings to draw on, or credit that enables them to borrow money, and these circumstances are usually more frequent at upper income levels."[29]

Dissavings that occur in one year as a result of, say, the purchase of a house or a major consumer durable good, must be followed by periods of savings required to make up for the dissavings. Such periods vary in length from two or three years to repay indebtedness incurred to purchase an automobile, to as long as twenty-five years to repay a mortgage on a house. Such payments require the individual to save, with the rate of savings predetermined by contractual obligations.

In brief, then, advertising, particularly that of the consumer variety, is directed at persuading the individual to spend more and to save less. But other types of advertising encourage individuals directly to save more, or indirectly via contractual undertakings following a period of dissavings. The effect of the former could be said to be anti-economic development, while the effect of the latter could be claimed to be pro-economic development.

Regrettably, this is still an oversimplification of a complex process. Rising consumer spending induces businessmen to expand productive capacity, which can be realized only through making necessary capital expenditures. Investment in turn contributes to both economic growth and economic development. Thus one arrives at a circular flow of reasoning—in essence a reflection of the interrelationship of the various income and expenditure streams that ebb and flow unevenly with the passage of time.

Advertising and Economic Progress

Economic progress may be measured in the most aggregative way in terms of real Gross National Product per capita. This means that potentially the average person may have access to a greater amount of output (i.e., income) but whether in fact he obtains a greater piece of the bigger pie will depend on how the pie is divided.

Even if each individual were to get a greater piece of the larger pie, to judge whether economic progress has taken place will also depend on what that pie consists of. For Gross National Product may increase because government spends more money on defence and military pursuits. In that case, Gross National Product per capita in real terms may be up. But as a result of a shift in the disposition of Gross National Product, the consumer may be less well off.

Also, the economy may be devoting a larger proportion than usual to capital formation and the proportion of the nation's output devoted to consumer spending may decline. In that case, the consumer may be said to be *potentially* better off, for he can expect that at some future date the large investment expenditures made will pay off in terms of rising real incomes and access to a greater volume of consumer goods and services. But in terms of the welfare benefits obtained by the consumer in the year in which the large capital expenditures are made, he may not be better off, even though Gross National Product in real terms per capita may be up.

Instead of measuring economic progress in terms of changes in real Gross National Product per capita, we may use changes in the volume of personal expenditures on consumer goods and services per capita as a measure. While this measurement indicates the progress the average individual in society makes through obtaining access to an increased volume of consumer goods and services, it still falls short because it limits the assessment to a quantity of output obtainable.

No allowance is made for (1) changes in the quality of goods and services becoming available, though presumably some of the changes would be reflected in the increase of the price level, (2) changes in consumer satisfaction obtained from greater access to more and better material comforts, and (3) changes in individual attitudes toward work—which facilitates the earning of income and the making of consumer purchases—and leisure—which increases non-material satisfaction and thus presents an antidote to the materialistic instincts of North American society.

Allowing for the difficulties of delineating and measuring economic progress adequately, the question arises: Does advertising contribute to economic progress or does it hinder it?

If economic progress is measured in terms of increases in consumer spending on goods and services in constant dollars per capita, then the basic point at issue is: How does advertising contribute to an increase in real consumer spending in aggregate? If it does, and if the population rises less rapidly than consumer spending in real terms, then outlays on consumer goods and services per capita would rise and economic progress as defined above would take place.

Against this, if all that advertising does is to persuade people to buy one commodity instead of another without contributing to a rise in consumer spending in aggregate to a level higher than it would have reached without advertising, then the latter would not appear to be a factor in raising consumer spending per capita and thus contributing to economic progress.

But even in this case there exists the possibility that advertising might have contributed to an upgrading in consumer satisfaction without increasing aggregate and per capita spending. Should this be considered as a form of economic progress?

To deal with the latter point first, assume that advertising convinces more people of the benefits of taking vacations and enjoying leisure activities, e.g., fishing, hunting, and golf, and that this fortifies their desire to work fewer hours per week. Assume further that productivity rises sufficiently to make up for the decline in the number of hours worked, that Gross National Product in real terms rises at the same rate as population, and Gross National Product per capita remains the same for two accounting periods. Assuming further that the ratio of consumer expenditures to Gross National Product is not altered, consumer expenditures per capita would also remain unchanged.

On the basis of Gross National Product per capita or consumer expenditures per capita, assuming unchanged price levels, the data would indicate that no economic progress has taken place. But in fact society is better off and the average consumer has improved his way of life. He has been able to obtain greater satisfaction from the division of time between work and leisure.

Similarly, people may be able to obtain greater satisfaction from switching from the purchase of one commodity to another without any change in the level of total spending on consumer goods and services. A person who gives up smoking and starts eating more may obtain greater satisfaction from this shift in his expenditure pattern, partly because he satisfies his conscience and partly because he replaces one satisfaction with another to which he attaches greater value.

To the extent that advertising contributes to a change in consumer wants and the manner in which these are met, it contributes to economic progress if the latter is more broadly defined to include any improvement in the over-all level of satisfaction obtained by individuals from a given volume of consumer spending.

To turn now to the more complex issue: Does advertising contribute to an increase in consumer spending in aggregate?

Ever since Keynes tied consumption "rigidly and passively . . . to income,"[30] by saying that the "propensity to consume is a fairly stable function so that, as a rule, the amount of aggregate consumption mainly depends on the amount of aggregate income,"[31] many economists have accepted the premise of a fairly stable consumption function over a *long* period of time. But some economists have questioned the premise and have said "quite flatly that the relation is not stable, except perhaps in the very limited sense of a tendency for consumption to hold in a certain relation to income over the long run."[32]

Some economists take a middle-of-the-road approach, declaring that

empirical evidence on the consumption-income relationship . . . suggests that disposable income is by far the most important factor influencing consumption spending. More specifically, it suggests that disposable income is of far greater importance in explaining consumption on a decade-to-decade basis than it is on a year-to-year basis . . . . [or] on a quarter-to-quarter basis. . . . The evidence clearly points to the presence of factors other than income that influence the amount that consumers spend in any year. While the income factor deserves and has received the major attention, the other factors are by no means of such little importance that they can be overlooked.[33]

Keynes himself made the point that many factors other than changes in levels of income affect levels of consumer spending, both objective and subjective. Examples of the former include fluctuations in prices, changes in tax rates and interest rates, and variations in the distribution of incomes. Examples of the latter include subjective needs and habits of the spending units, which, in turn, are affected not only by economic factors, but also by social and cultural forces.

Since the publication of the *General Theory*, the list of factors affecting consumer spending in aggregate has been greatly expanded to cover such variables as psychological forces, including income and price expectations, and the degree of consumer confidence, as well as such elements as changes in the holding of consumer assets, terms and availability of consumer credit, size of spending units, development of new and improved consumer goods and services, variations in educational standards and institutional organizations, the effectiveness of persuasion through the increasingly sophisticated use of the mass media, etc.

Empirical investigations conducted since Keynes was writing have established the existence of a fair degree of stability in the marginal propensity to consume. Still, most economists do not necessarily regard, as Professor Burns put it, the Keynesian "consumption function as fixed, but . . . they attach slight importance to its wanderings."[34] Some of these "wanderings" may be substantial, particularly if the measurement is reversed from the propensity to consume to the propensity to save, that is, the relationship between personal savings and personal disposable income in a given time period.[35]

For example, the ratio of personal savings to personal disposable income in the United States rose from 5.5 per cent, the average for the period 1959–1964, to 7.1 per cent in 1967, an increase in the savings to income ratio of about one-third over the period of a few years.[36] The Council of Economic Advisers lists a number of reasons for this significant increase in the savings ratio. These include: the purchase of large amounts of government bonds, the introduction of the Medicare system, which made it unnecessary to reduce savings to pay for health services, and the desire on the part of many individuals to increase their savings following acceleration of prices.[37] The Council concludes: "While few of these factors would imply a permanently higher saving rate, past evidence indicates that a reversion to a more normal rate is most likely to occur gradually rather than abruptly."[38]

In this connection, Professor Katona refers to a specific behavioural principle that helps to explain in part the significant rise in the personal savings ratio in the United States in recent years: "People exert a greater effort when they are close to their goal than when their goal appears hardly attainable. The findings help to explain the relatively high rate of liquid savings by consumers during the last few years in face of the widespread introduction of private pension plans."[39]

The difference in changes in the propensity to save and the propensity to consume over the last few years is about one and a half percentage points for the United States and three percentage points for Canada. With personal disposable income in the United States amounting to $545 billion in 1967, this difference was equivalent to about $8.2 billion. In Canada, with personal disposable income amounting to $42 billion in the same year, this difference involved about $1¼ billion.

Whether these deviations in the propensity to save and propensity to consume are minor "wanderings" to which neo-Keynesian scholars attach "slight importance," or whether such short-term variations are large enough to warrant the claim that there is some room for moving aggregate consumer spending up a notch or two on the income ladder, is a matter of opinion. But in absolute terms, the amounts involved appear to be large enough for businessmen to scramble for their share of expanding markets, and if possible for an increased share of such potential sales. Advertising is one of the tools of persuasion which businessmen use in their efforts to realize such objectives.

This point is made by Professor Backman:

> The total demand for all consumer goods is most significantly influenced by total disposable personal income. . . . However, as incomes rise, the pattern of spending changes gradually, with a smaller percentage used to buy foods and other necessities. . . .

Within an industry there may be changes in shares obtained by companies or for particular brands. . . . Advertising helps to influence these changes in shares and to expand *total* demand to some extent, particularly when new or improved products are made available. . . . When incomes are rising, there is also an *increased* opportunity to utilize advertising effectively.[40] [Italics added.]

Professor Julian Simon, in a stimulating article published in 1967, goes a step further. He submits that a logical case can be made "that advertising does affect aggregate spending" and that it does not.[41] In the latter case, "advertising merely affects how people *distribute* their expenditures, and does not affect the sum of them."

Professor Simon calls this the "spread-it-around" hypothesis. He explains: "This hypothesis implies that some constant proportion of income is 'taken off the top,' and what is left is spent according to the prevailing tastes of the spending unit."[42]

The two hypotheses are subjected to five tests: (1) a psychological test, (2) a quasi-experimental test, (3) a time series test, (4) a survey of expenditure test, and (5) an advertising expenditure test. The two main conclusions offered by Professor Simon are:

First, under certain circumstances, aggregate advertising will contribute to an increase in aggregate consumer spending. Advertising creates new wants (or brings latent wants[43] to the fore). In order to translate these wants into effective demand, people may do extra work (Professor Simon speaks of "moonlighting").[44] Additional income is earned with a proportion of this income spent on consumer goods and services "equal to the average propensity to consume." Thus, "advertising could have an important effect on spending without a visible change in the consumption function or even with an apparent decrease in the *proportion* spent."[45] Professor Simon mentions that education may have similar effects since it leads to higher incomes, a proportion of which becomes available for consumer spending.

Second, "the considerable stability in the average and marginal long-run propensities to consume over many decades is consistent with a spread-it-around theory" of the effect of advertising. Professor Simon makes the further point that some research work in the field of advertising involving time series analysis carried on at the University of Illinois offers some "slight indication . . . . that advertising is related to consumption."[46]

Anti-Progress Effect of Advertising

So far the discussion has centered around the contribution that advertising may make to enhance economic progress. But some of the effects may work in the opposite direction. In fact many arguments are presented on moral, social, and economic grounds that advertising affects human progress adversely.

One study lists a total of 33 adverse economic effects.[47] Another study lists about a dozen unfavourable social, personal, and moral effects of advertising.[48]

The defenders of advertising claim that many of the criticisms are unfounded, exaggerated, or unproven. And the debate continues unabated both at the professional and non-professional levels. Among the academics, the critics have the advantage of greater numbers and the support of some of the leading theoreticians, while those trying to steer the debate among more realistic lines sadly lack empirical evidence to test alternative hypotheses put forward, as Professor Simon's article so vividly demonstrates.

Some official comments are critical of certain aspects of advertising, for example, the effects which advertising may have on industrial concentration[49] and in boosting prices to consumers, with large profits accruing to big business which uses substantial amounts of advertising to market differentiated products.[50]

One of the most critical assessments of the economic and social role of advertising has been formulated by the Labour Party in Great Britain, which with a Labour Government in office, had considerable influence on public thinking on this subject. The report by this group recommends a variety of measures to curb advertising, including several suggestions to control advertising practices.[51]

But not all official or semi-official comments are so critical. A recent Commission of Enquiry in Canada concluded that many of the criticisms levelled against advertising had little foundation in fact or in theory, and that, provided adequate safeguards are taken "to prevent misuse of advertising in particular cases," no justification could be advanced "for any comprehensive set of controls such as special taxes on advertising, beyond the normal setting and definition of a broad legal and operational environment."[52]

The Commission went on record further to say:

> Where advertising accompanies, and is part of an uncompetitive industry structure it will generally be necessary to attack the sources of market power directly, thereby vitiating the usefulness of advertising in fortifying positions of power. To attack only advertising could well drive firms which do not face market competition into more devious avenues of persuasion.[53]

The Commission recommended that there be established in Canada an agency with functions similar to those of the United States Federal Trade Commission "with power to force advertisers to restrain or modify their announcements when these announcements are unacceptable in terms of honesty, adequacy, taste, or such other characteristics as can be agreed upon."[54]

CONCLUSION

The main theme of this paper has been Professor Sandage's challenging phrase: "Advertising, the institution of abundance."

There are two aspects of relating advertising to abundance.

One is to expand the economy's capacity to produce goods and services, with some of this potential taken out in the form of rising material satisfaction (improvement in the standard of living) and part of it in terms of increasing non-material satisfaction (expansion of leisure time). As the nation's wealth-creating capabilities expand, people must have the will and the knowledge, and they must exert the necessary efforts, to make full and effective use of their productive potential.

Advertising can assist in expanding both *potential* and *actual* Gross National Product. If potential Gross National Product expands at a fast pace and actual Gross National Product is close to potential Gross National Product, then the economy would be operating at or near a full-employment level and travelling along a rapid growth path.

Advertising can assist the growth of potential Gross National Product in a variety of ways. It can contribute to improvement of the quality of the labour force and its expansion in numbers, to the introduction of innovations, to increases in productivity leading to price reductions or slowdown of potential price increases, or stimulate a rise in personal savings.

The other aspect, using Professor Sandage's phrase, involves stretching "the wants of consumers, both for private and public goods and services." There is in this phrase a faint resemblance to Galbraith's theory of the social balance, which would channel more economic efforts into the provision of needed public services as a balance to large expenditures made on many trifling private goods and services, heavily promoted under the slogan of the "American Way of Life."

In looking at the social and economic functions performed by advertising, Professor Sandage and Professor Galbraith may be poles apart. Still, both men acknowledge that there is an urgent need to make the most effective and constructive use of the fabulous productive capacity of the United States.

Both scholars share the same objective although they differ on philosophical grounds and in matters of methodology.

Stretching consumer wants can be said to cover an array of activities, from showing consumers how existing wants can be met more effectively to creating new wants through demonstration, information, and persuasion, from arousing curiosity to try new things, to education which raises the capacity and the will to experiment and alters the sense of values from one generation to another, from one social strata to another, and from one ideology to another.

To the extent that advertising affects want creation and want change, it can have a fundamental effect on the will of society to devote its efforts to material pursuits. It is an essential function of advertising to persuade consumers to buy, and businessmen do not deny that persuasion, and not information, is the main reason they employ advertising. Once growing consumer wants are translated into effective demand, markets expand, businessmen profit, the economy prospers, and continuing economic growth and development take place.

But not all types of advertising serve such constructive purposes of making both the consumer and the businessman happy. There are some instances—critics claim there are many—when advertising involves social waste, misguides the consumer, and slows down economic progress.

Claims of disutility of advertising range all the way from shifting the decision-making process in the case of highly advertised products from the timid consumer to big business, to reducing competition and strengthening the firms which need it least—the successful oligopolists. Other adverse effects cited include unnecessarily high prices for some products brandishing trivial differentiation, and profits that rise with increasing advertising expenditures.[55]

Advertising brings many benefits to the economy. It also brings disutility to the consumer. On balance, the former appear to outweigh the latter, for if they did not, sooner or later as a result of public pressures, government would take action to curb and control advertising.

Still, the criticism of advertising is mounting at the academic, political, and public levels. Why is this so?

Is it that advertising is not only an "instrument of abundance" but also an "instrument of ignorance"?

Perhaps one of the answers why there is such a lack of understanding of the effects of advertising, the growing public debate notwithstanding, is that there is no systematic and continuous effort to throw light on the subject in an objective and professional manner. Research in the field of advertising by the academics is still in its infancy. And what goes under the name of research in the advertising industry are largely efforts to assess the effectiveness of advertising specific commodities, and not the economic effects of advertising.

It is not enough to find out why people buy or do not buy a particular product and how many people read newspaper advertisements or are exposed to commercials on radio and television. There is also need to learn why people behave the way they do and what some of the key factors are that lead to the making of genuine consumer decisions.[56]

NOTES

[1] "Education and the Advertising Industry," in *Interdisciplinary Approaches to Advertising Education*, Occasional Papers in Advertising, Vol. I, No. 1, Jan. 1966, p. 94 (American Academy of Advertising). Professor Sandage drew on the writings of David M. Potter, who used the phrase "The Institution of Abundance: Advertising" in his book *People of Plenty: Economic Abundance and the American Character* (Chicago: University of Chicago Press, 1961), pp. 166 ff.

[2] *Ibid.*

[3] *The New Industrial State* (Boston: Houghton Mifflin Company, 1967), p. 210.

[4] *Economic Analysis*, Microeconomics, Vol. I (4th ed.; New York: Harper and Row, 1966), pp. 513, 514.

[5] *American Industry: Structure, Conduct, Performance* (Englewood Cliffs, N.J.: Prentice-Hall, Inc., 1964), p. 102.

[6] "The Economic Aspects of Advertising," *The Review of Economic Studies* (1950–1951), No. 45, p. 6.

[7] "Advertising in Today's Economy," in *The Canadian Quandary* (Toronto: The McGraw-Hill Company of Canada Limited, 1963), pp. 280, 281.

[8] *The New Industrial State*, p. 326.

[9] *Ibid.*, p. 293.

[10] In the type of "mixed" enterprise that characterizes the economies of the United States and Canada, "the choices of consumers determine both the prices and the quantities of goods produced and consumed." But the concept of consumer sovereignty is broader than that for it may be said to apply "equally well to choices in regard to the individual's output of services," that is, occupational choices, and to the decisions which individuals make to save or to consume with their effects on the over-all rate of capital accumulation. (See Kenneth E. Boulding, *Principles of Economic Policy* (London: Staples Press, 1963), pp. 142, 144.)

[11] *The New Industrial State*, p. 71.

[12] "In a dynamic and progressive society, the consumer needs to learn how to spend his increasing income and can afford to pay for information and advice; he can also afford the waste of errors and experimentation." (See Harry G. Johnson, "Apologia for Ad Men," in *The Canadian Quandary* (Toronto: The McGraw-Hill Company of Canada Limited, 1963), p. 290.)

[13] The incidence of poverty still continues to be heavy though growing affluence has brought some decrease. The proportion of households in the United States defined as living in poverty decreased over the period 1959–1966 as follows: Non-farm, from 22.5 per cent to 17.6 per cent, and farm, from 40.9 per cent to 20.8 per cent. (See *Economic Report of the President, together with the Annual Report of the Council of Economic Advisers*, transmitted to the Congress February 1968 (Washington, D.C.: U.S. Government Printing Office, 1968, p. 143.) More recently, a *Report of the Citizens' Crusade Against Poverty*, headed by Walter Reuther, President of the United Autoworkers,

published in Washington in April 1968, claimed that some 10 million Americans living in twenty states of the Union were suffering from starvation. This led Senator George McGovern to introduce a resolution calling for a special Senate Committee to find ways to end "the paradox of want and starvation in the most affluent society in the history of mankind." For a discussion of the state of poverty in Canada, see O. J. Firestone, *Problems of Economic Growth*, (Ottawa: University of Ottawa Press, 1965, pp. 22–31).

[14] The term "realizable" is used to indicate that in the present stage of the social sciences, even the most effective instruments of economic policy will not fully eradicate poverty and deprivation, though they may contribute materially to a further reduction in the number of people living at below-subsistence standards and failing to find adequate economic opportunities to be able to lead a life of human dignity.

[15] That is, for more education rather than for greater usage of drugs, and for better housing than for more gambling.

[16] This exposition of concepts is from O. J. Firestone, "Education and Economic Development—The Canadian Case," *The Review of Income and Wealth* (September, 1968).

[17] *Principles of Economic Policy*, p. 23.

[18] See discussion of "The Theory of Social Balance" in John Kenneth Galbraith, *The Affluent Society* (Boston: Houghton Mifflin Company, 1958), pp. 251–269.

[19] *Report of the Royal Commission on Consumer Problems and Inflation*, The Prairie Provinces Cost Study Commission, Province of Alberta, Province of Manitoba, Province of Saskatchewan (Regina, Sask.: Queen's Printer, 1968), p. 260.

[20] In this context, economic growth is taken to mean the continuing expansion of output over a longer period of time starting from a full employment or near full employment position. In this sense, an increase of output during the recovery period from the trough of the business cycle would not be considered economic growth. Economists who do not make this distinction describe as economic growth *any* increase in real Gross National Product.

[21] Jules Backman devotes part of a chapter in his book to the subject "Advertising and Economic Growth." He refers in particular to the effect of advertising in "complementing the efforts to create new and improved products through expenditures for research and development." (See *Advertising and Competition* (New York: New York University Press, 1967), p. 22.)

[22] To the extent that increased education and training contributes to productivity improvements, this in turn would affect the rate of economic development.

[23] Joseph A. Schumpeter, *Business Cycles* (New York: McGraw-Hill Book Company, Inc, 1939), I, 84.

[24] O. J. Firestone, *The Economic Implications of Advertising* (Toronto: Methuen Publications, 1967), pp. 94, 95.

[25] See Jules Backman, *Advertising and Competition*, pp. 42–46.

[26] Donald F. Turner, "Advertising and Competition," Paper at the Briefing Conference on Federal Controls of Advertising and Promotion, sponsored by the Federal Bar Association, etc., Washington, D.C., June 2, 1966, pp. 2, 3.

[27] Mark S. Massel, *Competition and Monopoly* (Washington, D.C.: The Brookings Institution, 1962), p. 199. (See also *Advertising and Competition*, *op. cit.*, p. 46.)

[28] George Katona, *Psychological Analysis of Economic Behavior* (New York: McGraw-Hill Book Company, Inc., 1963), pp. 161–165.

[29] *Ibid.*, p. 161.

[30] A. F. Burns, "Keynesian Economics Once Again," *Review of Economics and Statistics*, 29 (1947), 261.

[31] J. M. Keynes, *The General Theory of Employment, Interest and Money* (New York: Harcourt, Brace and World, Inc., 1965), p. 96.

[32] Maurice W. Lee, *Macroeconomics, Fluctuations, Growth and Stability* (Homewood, Ill.: Richard D. Irwin, Inc., 1963), p. 35.

[33] Edward Shapiro, *Macroeconomic Analysis* (New York: Harcourt, Brace and World, Inc., 1966), pp. 215, 216.

[34] "Keynesian Economics Once Again," p. 261.

[35] Professor Katona questions the adequacy of the empirical tests on the basis of aggregate economic analysis using two main variables, income levels and income changes. He observes: "In order to understand how and why the community's propensity to save changes, we cannot rely on time series of aggregate data alone. We must also study the developments in terms of the behavior of the units which constitute the economy, that is, we must proceed with studies on the micro-economic level." (See *Psychological Analysis of Economic Behavior, op. cit.*, pp. 136, 137.)

[36] In Canada, the ratio of personal savings to personal disposable income rose from 6.5 per cent in 1964, to 9.6 per cent in 1967, or by over two-fifths. (See *National Accounts, Income and Expenditure, 1966,* and *1967* (Ottawa: Dominion Bureau of Statistics, 1967 and 1968.).)

[37] *Economic Report of the President, op. cit.*, p. 49.

[38] *Ibid.*, p. 50.

[39] "On the Function of Behavioral Theory and Behavioral Research in Economics," *The American Economic Review*, LVIII (March, 1968), 148.

[40] *Advertising and Competition*, pp. 12, 13.

[41] "The Effect of Advertising on the Propensity to Consume," *Kyklos*, XX, Fasc. 4 (1967), 959.

[42] *Ibid.*, p. 951.

[43] Some professionals do not agree with the view that advertising "creates" new wants. For example, John Hobson, described in *The Observer* as probably the leading expert on marketing in Great Britain, advances the concept of latent wants. He makes the point: "Advertising is accused of creating wants. This is not a true picture; advertising evokes and activates latent wants which people never realized they had the means of satisfying." (See John Hobson, "The Social and Economic Context of Advertising," Lecture I of the Three Cantor Lectures, *The Influences and Techniques of Modern Advertising* (London: The Royal Society for the Encouragement of Arts, Manufactures and Commerce, March 2, 1964, Reprint, p. 5.) The question of whether advertising creates or does not create new wants, is discussed further in Firestone, *The Economic Implications of Advertising*, pp. 88–92.

[44] Professor Simon could also have mentioned overtime, or additional members of the household joining the labour force, e.g., a married woman, to afford greater comforts or to purchase a major consumer durable good or a house.

[45] Simon, "The Effect of Advertising on the Propensity to Consume," p. 954.

[46] *Ibid.*, p. 959.

[47] Firestone, *The Economic Implications of Advertising*, pp. 20, 21. The 33 criticisms of advertising do not exhaust the subject.

[48] *Report of the Royal Commission on Consumer Problems and Inflation*, pp. 258–266.

[49] Turner, "Advertising and Competition," *op. cit.*, and "Advertising and Competition: Restatement and Amplification," Address before the Annual Advertising Government Relations Conference, Washington, D.C., February 8, 1967.

[50] *Statement* of Dr. Willard F. Mueller, Director, Bureau of Economics, Federal Trade Commission, before the Monopoly Subcommittee of the Select Committee on Small Business, United States Senate, Washington, D.C., January 18, 1968, and *Supplement to Statement* of Dr. Willard F. Mueller made before the same Committee, April 2, 1968.

[51] *Report of a Commission of Enquiry into Advertising, The Labour Party,* (Reith Report), London, England, 1966, pp. 186–200.

[52] *Report of the Royal Commission on Consumer Problems and Inflation,* pp. 269, 270.

[53] *Ibid.,* p. 270.

[54] *Ibid.*

[55] "The companies which are most successful in achieving a highly differentiated product are able to charge higher prices and make higher profits than the less advantaged companies. . . . There is a strong positive relationship between the absolute amount of an industry's advertising and its average profit rates." (See *Supplement to Statement,* of Dr. Willard F. Mueller, pp. 15, 16.)

[56] Professor Katona makes the point "that admonitions and exhortations alone, even if reiterated over and over again through the radio, in newspapers or posters, are not the best means of influencing people's behavior substantially over an extensive period." (See *Psychological Analysis of Economic Behavior,* p. 288.)

CHAPTER 4

Science and Advertising Theory

by Wendell R. Smith

Dr. Smith is dean of the School of Business Administration, University of Massachusetts, and chairman of the National Marketing Advisory Committee, U.S. Department of Commerce. He formerly was president of the Marketing Science Institute, professor of marketing at the Wharton School of Finance and Commerce, University of Pennsylvania, staff vice president for marketing development, Radio Corporation of America, a partner in Alderson and Sessions, and head of the Department of Marketing, State University of Iowa. He also is a former president of the American Marketing Association. In 1962 he was elected to the Distribution Hall of Fame.

I am highly honored to take part in this C. H. Sandage Symposium being held in honor of one who has made substantial contributions to advertising as a science, a discipline, an art, and a way of life. It has been my privilege to be associated with Sandy in many ventures over the years and to observe the singular, and sometimes stubborn, way in which he has insisted that advertising phenomena merit application of the most vigorous techniques of analysis available. His work thus far, and I am sure it will continue for many years, has been a major factor in stimulating students, scholars, and practitioners in this field, which he asserts is entitled to first-class citizenship among the business disciplines.

Lesser men in the academic community have been dissuaded

from serious work in the field of advertising by the never fully resolved jurisdictional dispute as to whether advertising belongs in the Business School, the School of Communications, or both. Some have even argued that it doesn't belong either place by virtue of the fact that criticism of the advertising function has long been a popular indoor sport. I submit that the man we honor at this symposium has done more than any other one person to refute this assertion.

When I was invited to present a paper on the subject "Science and Advertising Theory," I accepted immediately because of the significance of the occasion, but it was not until a few weeks ago when I faced up to the serious task of preparing these remarks that I became fully aware of the magnitude of the assignment. Obviously, the topic could be approached in a variety of ways. The entire symposium could be devoted to an interesting, but probably unproductive, discussion of the semantic issues involved. That I have elected not to do. Rather, I would like to do what comes naturally for a marketing man and offer a few observations as to where we now stand in the development of the theoretical and scientific components of advertising, which is itself an important component of the over-all marketing process.

My thinking about advertising was profoundly influenced by the first marketing professor with whom I came in contact, the late William F. Bristol of the University of Iowa. Professor Bristol viewed advertising and its development as a key factor in the marketing counterpart of the Industrial Revolution. "Advertising," he said, "is mechanized selling. We develop a sales message, we mass produce it, and send it out through the available and relevant media." But advertising is more than that. To me it is that mix of art, science, creativity, and good fortune that enables us to communicate persuasively about goods and services so as to accelerate and expand their purchase and use by consumers and other users. It is a pervasive force in our economy that, strangely enough, is often viewed skeptically by its users, whereas its opponents are confident of its effectiveness.

NEW TOOLS AND CONCEPTS

The historians of this decade in the development of the science or discipline of marketing may well characterize it as the decade of the search for consensus on what is truly fundamental in the marketing and advertising processes. This quest for an understanding of fundamentals has been prompted by many things, among them the advent of new research tools and techniques that make it feasible to attempt to construct models and to simulate discrete marketing activities and the systems of which those activities are part. Because the advantages and gains springing from these methodological advances are so promising, so exciting, and so essential, many traditional controversies have become subordinated to the common drive for development of the principles and concepts necessary to enable marketing to consolidate and hold the gains it has made.

We are even arriving at some tentative conclusions, as one of the Marketing Science Institute studies pointed out, as to possible resolution of the classic sales-measures–versus–communications-measures argument.

Some of the newer analytical techniques force us to recognize the important distinctions between the various business decisions concerned with advertising. Although sales measures may be the best available lowest common denominator upon which to base decisions involving allocation of the marketing dollar among various marketing tools (including advertising), communications measures may be more useful in determining how best to spend the dollar advertising gets.

In the decade of the sixties we can observe the convergence of a number of developments, both in the environment and within marketing and advertising, that taken together have the power to bring about profound changes in what we do and how we do it. Even some of our economist friends are beginning to recognize that freedom of consumer choice, freedom of choice of occupation, and freedom of investment are what marketing and the market economy are all about.

The history of any science or discipline is likely to reveal a continuing switch in emphasis from fragmentation and analysis, on the one hand, to synthesis and generalization on the other. It is my belief that marketing and advertising have now reached the point where the foundation of analysis is probably adequate for us to understand something of the marketing and advertising process or system as a whole. Now, what are some of the factors that have brought us to this threshold?

There are at least four of primary importance: *First,* we must mention the emergence and development of the techniques of marketing and advertising research that have given us the necessary data upon which to build. *Second,* we are only now coming to realize the magnitude of the revolution being caused by significant advances in transportation and communication. It becomes more obvious every day that many of our concepts in marketing assume the use of rail and steamship transportation rather than the jet airplane, and thus fail to take into account the increased reliability and low cost of world-wide telecommunications. *Third,* there is the computer, be it friend or foe, with its seemingly insatiable appetite for data and information and—more important—its insistence upon the conceptual and mathematical models of processes and systems. These models are the software without which the computer cannot perform at its highest level of utility—that of putting a multiplier on the mind of man, just as the first Industrial Revolution put a multiplier on the muscles of man. *Fourth,* these factors combine to produce a "knowledge explosion," as we old-line marketers are joined by the operations researchers, the behavioral scientists, the environmentalists and others interested in our problems.

TRENDS INFLUENCING MARKETING AND ADVERTISING THEORY

Now, let's attempt to isolate the impact that these developments are having and will have on marketing and advertising thinking.

The *first* of these—and in many respects the most important —may be described as the *decline of the dichotomy and the rise of the continuum.* Let me illustrate. When the classical economists designated two kinds of goods—those immediately ready for consumption, or consumer goods, and those to be used in production, or capital goods—the idea of emphasizing the *differences* between the marketing of consumer goods and industrial goods was given its theoretical foundation. Marketing people immediately concluded that if there were two kinds of goods, there must be two kinds of marketing; thus, the dichotomy of consumer marketing and industrial marketing was established. For many years this dichotomy served us well in that, generally speaking, consumer goods were characterized by high frequency of purchase, low unit cost, and relatively high perishability, whereas industrial goods represented more substantial investments and much longer periods of useful life. Today, however, your garage and kitchen and mine contain many items that bear a strong resemblance to industrial goods, both in terms of their investment and durability and in terms of our behavior when we buy them.

Similarly, a substantial and perhaps increasing number of industrial goods are moving to market through channels of distribution that strongly resemble the channels for consumer goods. This is the direct result of the increasing complexity of products, which necessitates the assembly of components from many sources, as opposed to relatively simple conversion of raw materials into useful goods. In addition, marketing communications for these goods are tending, albeit slowly, toward increased use of impersonal media, as in the case of consumer marketing. We have now, and probably always will have, hard-core, clearly distinguishable consumer marketing at one end of the continuum and hard-core industrial marketing at the other. However, we are becoming increasingly aware of the expanding gray area between these extremes where the most effective marketing program has some characteristics traditionally associated with consumer marketing and some traditionally associated with industrial marketing. Therefore, today, the accent is less on differences and distinctions and more on *similarities*. Out of this can come nothing but good.

The point may also be illustrated in connection with the marketing of goods as opposed to the marketing of services.

Daily one can observe the increasing extent to which services that were once individually tailored to the consumer are being standardized, packaged, and marketed in the true sense of the term. Your homeowner's insurance policy is a case in point. On the other hand, as household appliances become more fully capable of the independent performance of certain tasks, for example, the automatic washer, they are being marketed more in terms of the service they can perform than in terms of their product characteristics. Here, too, the continuum is replacing the dichotomy.

Even more obvious is the situation with reference to domestic marketing versus international marketing. Today an American marketing manager who does not concern himself with the international market is asking for trouble. He may ignore developing competition from abroad that will give him difficulties in the home market, and at the same time he may be committing the equally unpardonable sin of overlooking opportunities for his company's products, services, or capabilities in markets outside of the United States. For many years one of the cardinal sins of American overseas marketing was that of underestimating differences and of assuming that marketing strategies successful at home were assured of success abroad. Perhaps we err in the opposite direction today by overemphasizing differences in failing to realize the increasing adaptability of *strategies* developed in this country to foreign markets in the more developed countries of the world. It appears that dichotomist thinking is, or should be, on the way out.

Second I would like to identify the trend toward declining interest in and relevance of functional discreteness in marketing. By that I mean that marketing specialists who define their areas of specialization narrowly are less in demand and occupy places of lesser importance than those who are more fully aware of the interdependence of functions and, hence, more capable of seeing the big picture, the process, or the system that is at work. In a recent speech at Stanford University, Robert Sarnoff, President of RCA, emphasized the need for executives who are equally at home with "a computer print-out and an advertising layout." Examples of this trend are not difficult to come by.

Some specialists in operations research and related quantitative techniques who have become interested in the application of their skills to marketing phenomena have tended to lavish unwarranted attention on minor marketing issues because the available data fit the model and because they are unable to discriminate between issues in terms of their importance in the marketing program. These same people, however, teamed with marketing generalists with developed diagnostic capabilities, are at a premium because of the significant contributions they can make both to marketing theory and to marketing practice.

It is interesting and frightening to speculate as to whether the increased marketing orientation of managements in our major companies, or the rather widespread acceptance of the marketing management concept, will in the long run increase or decrease in relative importance of marketing personnel per se. One may argue that marketing executives will be listened to with greater attention by the top management people in their companies than they were formerly. On the other hand, one can cite instances where general management has begun to devote personal attention to marketing issues, deeming them too important to delegate to others. Simultaneously, we hear more each day about "integrated management," a development born of the expectation that the computer and associated information systems will shortly make it possible for top management people to concern themselves simultaneously with company and system-wide issues because of their enhanced understanding of their interrelationships. With regard to advertising, one notes in the literature a growing interest in how the total advertising process works, associated perhaps with some decline of interest in the components of that process, such as copy, media, and so forth. If this is true, the implications for education and manpower development are great indeed.

The *third* trend I would like to mention is, in a sense, a product of the other two, namely, an increasing interest in theory. Not too many years ago, the word "theory" was used by businessmen primarily in the context of the statement, "It may be all right in theory, but it won't work in practice." However, at a meeting of the Marketing Science Institute Board of

Trustees, when the first project in the area of marketing theory was being discussed, one member of that board, who was the chairman of a major company, said: "I don't know exactly what you mean by marketing theory, but what I urgently need in my position is a frame of reference within which to position and interrelate the many decisions about advertising and marketing that I am called upon to make." This, to me, is the most eloquent statement of the role of theory in the management process that I have ever heard.

Why an increased interest in theory? Why is as much, or more, theoretical work being done in major business firms as in our colleges and universities? The plain truth is that theory has become practical and necessary as the basis for understanding the increasingly complex and computerized world in which we live and work. I could talk about this particular point all day, but suffice it to say that theory is, among other things, one way of analyzing and recording experience so that it can be communicated from one person to another and accumulated for educational and training purposes. Furthermore, theoretical concepts are the raw material out of which models can be constructed and the means by which systems can be understood. It is no longer necessary to apologize for having an interest in theoretical considerations. One needs only to think for a moment of the satellites buzzing over our heads to realize the close interrelationship that exists today between the theoretical and the practical.

A WORD ABOUT EDUCATION FOR MARKETING AND ADVERTISING

I think I have already anticipated many of the points that might be made about the role of marketing and advertising education in providing the business community with the capabilities that will be required in the years that lie ahead. Our educational institutions must lead the business community, rather than lag behind it, in accepting the implications of the irreversible trends that we see developing around us. We must make certain that students become familiar not only with today's techniques of analysis but with today's techniques of synthesis.

The marketing and advertising men of the future must be at home in the world of models and simulations. They must be aware of the dynamism of the system in which they work and the essentiality of continuing to study and to grow throughout their careers. They must be excited by change, not threatened by it. They must accept the fact that adaptability to change is becoming a primary requisite of success—that capability is coming to be thought of as a flow of competence rather than an inventory of information and know-how. This is the challenge that makes it imperative that the academic and business communities work together more closely than ever before.

II. FRONTIERS OF ADVERTISING RESEARCH

CHAPTER 5

Colonizing the Frontiers of Advertising Research

by Sherwood Dodge

The late Mr. Dodge was president of the Advertising Research Foundation. He previously served as marketing vice president, Toilet Articles Division, Colgate-Palmolive Company, executive vice president, Fletcher D. Richards agency, vice president, marketing, Foote, Cone & Belding, and director of research, Office of Price Administration. He was a past president of the Copy Research Council and co-author of The Engineering of Consent.

With all respect to the truly distinguished speakers in this symposium, I wonder if one day—perhaps even at an Advertising Research Foundation conference—some Professor Dunn will have the courage to summarize it by saying, "Well, gentlemen, the Frontiers of Advertising Research were perceptibly extended today; in twenty or thirty years, it is hoped, we will be able to develop direct supply lines and communications with these new outposts!"

Not being a military man, I am a little diffident about using strategic or tactical imagery, but I seem to remember some law relating advances to follow-through capabilities, the idea being that there had to be some balance between the energies of forward thrust and the logistics of supply.

Perhaps Carl Sandburg was speaking of the same imbalance when he wrote of the baseball pitcher who had "lots of speed, but no control." This fellow may have been a bonus baby, but he never made it in the major leagues.

IMBALANCE BETWEEN HYPOTHESIS AND VERIFICATION

What I want to talk to you about is the shocking imbalance between hypothesis and verification, between theory and experimental evidence, in advertising research today. I regard it as such a serious problem in our industry that we are in danger of operating more from a base of supposition or outright mythology than from an authentically scientific base. Worse yet, we are in danger of being found out. If I am right that there is an increasing alienation between the advertising researcher and the advertising writers and decision-makers, it may now be later than we think.

"Alienation, did you say? Why, more money is being spent on advertising research than ever before!"

I say look again. More money is being spent on unvalidated procedural exercises that purport to evaluate media and copy. More money is being spent on individual rituals of testing, ostensibly to reduce corporate capital risk, but perhaps more often to reduce the personal risks of the decision-maker; to make up for a lack of generalizing power on effective advertising on the part of the agency, which has lost this initiative; or to meet the ego needs of marketing management, who believe research to be an "in" activity in the business community today, and are comforted that their companies are at least nominally so engaged.

Just last month, the man who has contributed more to the validation of research methods than any other of our generation—Alfred Politz—had this to say to the American Marketing Association:

> . . . research is increasingly used as a status symbol, proof of the modernity of the company which finances it. Research as a status symbol does not have to perform; it only has to exist. A symbol which is supposed to represent the real thing can easily become a substitute for the real thing. It is some sort of rule that a man takes off his hat for a female when he finds himself in a vehicle moving vertically; that is, an elevator. He does not have to do so if the vehicle moves horizontally, such as the subway. Taking off his hat in the elevator is intended to symbolize his respect for the female sex. After the man has freed himself of his

duty to manufacture the symbol by removing his hat, he goes to his office and hires the girl at a salary that is half what he would pay for a man performing the same function.

I mentioned a growing "alienation" between research and the operational advertising world, even though advertising research and the corporation appear to be properly married. If any two official bodies exist to disseminate knowledge of how advertising works, whether through media or copy, they would be the American Association of Advertising Agencies and the Association of National Advertisers.

We have examined their national conference programs for the last fifteen years, and the incidence of research speakers addressing themselves to copy or media research has slowly dwindled. My librarian told me that an analysis of 4A programs indicated that the last speaker to present research data having any bearing on how advertising works spoke in 1956, twelve long years ago. Somewhat appalled, I asked who this speaker was. It completely spoils the point I want to make to tell you that the librarian answered "It was you, Mr. Dodge." I should have preferred to make the point that the reason we haven't been asked back is because we have had nothing to say since then. Now it may be suggested that I made a very bad speech.

Since then, more time has been given to electronic data processing, but none to the validity of the inputs. And, increasing attention (and applause) has been given to copywriters who could build joke routines around the absurdities of their research environment. I call this evidence of alienation —and perhaps well deserved.

SHORTCOMINGS OF COMMERCIAL RESEARCH

A moment ago I spoke, possibly with some lack of charity, of the unvalidated procedural exercises that constitute the body of much of today's advertising research. I will soon get down to specifics, but this missing "something to say" to advertisers and agencies might well have consisted of some generalizations from the vast storehouse of commercial research experience. The accumulated experiments of such a relatively old firm as the Schwerin Organization might have produced more generalizations on what makes effective and ineffective advertising, even though using a pre-to-post technique that has yet to be validated after all these years. To be fair, periodic news bulletins did appear, some of them very interesting, though the burden of their presentation might be construed more in the service of sales than in the service of industry.

A newer organization, and seemingly a very prosperous one, Audience Studies, Inc., has yet to my knowledge to issue its first generalizing news bulletin. In fact, the most vocal of the generalists, Harry Wayne McMahan, produces some valuable insights from a taxonomical approach to TV commercials, and indeed, thinks very little of the capability of currently popular research techniques to predict a successful commercial. Just two years ago I was a witness to a surprising statement made by the copy research chief of one of our very largest agencies to its assembled account executives that "on balance, copy research probably did more good than harm." And, so far as media research is concerned, no one of the current syndicated services, with the exception of W. R. Simmons, has ever been formally reviewed by an objective body. Current rating services are "audited" by the Broadcast Rating Council, for procedural fulfillment, but no official body of research exists to determine the degree to which these procedures are meaningful.

I have been either a producer or a user of advertising research most of my business life. In my present job, I confront daily both research producers and users. It appears to me that while the frontiers of avant-garde research thinking have been expanding like an uncontained gas, the scientifically defensible, operating frontiers in business application have been shrinking. I regard it as a fact that management *expects* less of advertising research today than it did ten years ago. We have failed to validate, and we have failed to generalize —two activities essential to scientific effort. And, because researchers can speak to users only of intriguing, but limited, case histories, or promises of what some novel bit of advanced technology might someday perform, the ANA and the 4A's have not asked us back. As a former research-user member of both groups, I think I understand their limited interest in us.

All of the admired research statements have been made when we were talking to ourselves. We have really had very little worth saying to them—and they know it.

What I have called the shocking imbalance between prevailing techniques and validation can be illustrated by ten questions I will put to you now. Each of them is fundamental to the conduct of advertising research, as it is widely practiced today. It is my belief that no one of you can honestly answer any of them affirmatively.

1. Do you feel you have adequate evidence that attitude-change measurements predict subsequent purchase behavior in any field, say, package goods?

2. In TV commercial testing, have you been exposed to comparative results of the conventional pre-to-post response levels versus the comparison of response levels between matched samples of exposed and unexposed prospects?

3. Are you familiar with any substantial body of evidence comparing the pretesting of advertising using laboratory methods as compared with "real-life" field testing?

4. Do you feel that most of the important methodological questions in current services which use recall methods to estimate reach and/or frequency of total audience to media, have been satisfactorily disposed of?

5. Are you satisfied with the quality-control of field interviewing, in respect to honesty, training, general competence, and interviewer histories?

6. Do you feel we know enough about qualitative or non-sampling differences between interviews obtained by personal interview, by mail, or by telephone?

7. Are you generally familiar with the relationship between physiological measurements—whether pupillometry, basal skin response, etc.—and other criteria measurements of effective advertising?

8. Are you satisfied with the available body of knowledge in

respect to consumer diary problems resulting from either low cooperation rates or from reporting error?

9. Is there a useful body of evidence that will permit us to make sound intermedia comparisons in respect to cost per unit of effectiveness?

10. The personal survey technique appears to be well established. Have we sufficient evidence of areas in which subjective reports correspond or fail to correspond to observed behavior?

If you will agree that these ten questions are highly germane to current practice in advertising research, and if you find yourself less than satisfied with the evidence that might support an affirmative answer, then let us confront our real dilemma.

There is not one of these questions that is not susceptible to validated research procedures, based on present knowledge of design that is widely available in our field. I say "validation procedures" because the act of employing them frequently modifies the underlying hypotheses, which in turn requires further verification effort, etc., etc. But the first steps are clearly within our capability, and have been for more than a decade.

Well, how did we get ourselves into a situation where the methodological underpinnings of our most routine work is based on such broadly untested procedures?

In my remaining remarks I would like to suggest how we got into this predicament, what we must do now to extricate ourselves from it, and what professional as well as competitive rewards await us if we do.

GENESIS OF THE PROBLEM

I think the genesis of our problem lies in what you might call a "secret weapon" concept of research, which accounted for management's strong sponsorship of our early growth. Twenty-five years ago, both marketing and advertising research were far better developed in advertising agencies than they were in most advertiser organizations, and more developed here than in our universities.

The beautiful metonymy of sampling—of the part standing for the whole—captured both the imagination and the sales sense of advertising agents. Later, the controlled experiment became a kind of Promised Land that lay beyond the wilderness of advertising variables. It takes nothing away from the many sincere and dedicated advertising practitioners who saw a route to increased efficiency and reduced risk in these procedures, to also point out that research became a formidable agency selling tool. And, viewed as a competitive weapon, research mushroomed because it was both advertised and sold as a proprietary. It seldom if ever made a profit in itself. But, whatever values it added to the advertising product, the claims made for it did attract business.

As advertisers moved into this field, the "secret weapon" concept moved with it, and to this day some of the oldest, tiredest, and often most superannuated body of techniques are regarded by many top managements as matters of the highest security, not findings, mind you, but methods. This fact, of course, is widely known among college professors who have tried to augment their teaching with good case histories, no matter their willingness to disguise brand names.

This thesis can be dealt with much less superficially another time. It should be enough to say that the constant migration of research personnel from one company to another—let alone professional friendships—gave the security status of these secrets an even shorter life than the military expect of advanced weaponry, which some say is as little as three years. You might score one for professionalism in our group if it weren't for two countervailing forces which the "secret weapon" myth produced.

One, of course, is the great emphasis on novelty—new theories, new techniques, new insights—not only because these were highly salable, but also, because of the nature of the system, it was the simplest way for a researcher to draw attention to himself.

The second was cost. It was both easier and cheaper to put forth ten plausible techniques than it was to validate properly any one of them. While the great theorists in the physical and biological sciences were followed by whole armies of experimentalists to determine degrees of validity, not so in the upward and onward world of applied advertising research. The facts are that very few firms were able or willing to pay the substantial costs of methodological or validating research, and those very few which did were all the more likely to view it as a secret weapon. The system itself created a whole bibliography of scientific dropouts.

Thus, pressure for novelty in a proprietary environment on the one hand, and costs that were either unsupportable or indefensible from the viewpoint of the individual company, on the other, have brought us to a pass where the lack of tested or validated techniques and our inability or unwilling-ness to generalize from data at hand leave us a lore to pass on to our young, but hardly a science.

SUGGESTED SOLUTIONS

How we got into this predicament is relevant only to how we might work our way out of it. I have several thoughts in this area which I think may be constructive, and which I would like to share with you.

The first step, I believe, is to discuss this problem among ourselves, as professionals, to reach some consensus on the degree to which it is handicapping both our professional and business interests.

If such a consensus can be reached, then the next step is to begin a dialogue with management which

1. states the problem,
2. distinguishes between the secrecy properly attached to competitive research *findings* and the quasi-public nature of research *methods,*
3. acknowledges that the substantial costs of methodological research will probably not be returned by an advantage to a brand or group of brands, and
4. suggests the desirability of industry joint effort to produce methodological advances at affordable costs.

The latter suggestion should probably be accompanied by a list of recommended methodological studies, in order of their importance to the company concerned.

I think that management is ready to hear such a message, and that this undertaking has a high assay of success. For one thing, it will require an act of frankness and modesty on our part, which in some quarters will be wholly unexpected and refreshing. Confidence in the research director as a professional should be markedly elevated.

I recognize that there may be a few even in this audience who vastly underestimate the magnitude of the effort required, and who interpret these remarks as a self-serving statement of the Advertising Research Foundation. Let me say quickly that we could quadruple our efforts over the next five years in this area, and only scratch the surface.

The undone work is so formidable that it will require every form of cooperative resource: inter-company projects, initiated by like-minded research directors; cooperative studies of method, initiated by research houses; exploration of common opportunities by organizations such as the American Marketing Association or the Marketing Science Institute; and by qualified universities and colleges, whose help can be enlisted by grants for projects considerably beyond the normal scope or sophistication of most doctoral dissertations.

Indeed, I should hope that the Advertising Research Foundation would be very active in sweeping this methodological stable, and that through our publications, we might also serve as an information center for the programs of others as well as our own.

Our selfish interest, if we have one, is that our membership will be able to conduct private, competitive research from a more solid foundation than it now can, no matter who develops the knowledge. This should reflect itself in lower costs, less waste, and higher predictive power, any one of which should be welcomed by management.

PROSPECT FOR NEW FRONTIERS

This afternoon's topic relates to New Frontiers of Advertising Research. Someday, when I'm less fretful about our failure to colonize the Old Frontiers—when some balance is restored between the energies of forward thrust and the logistics of supply—I'd like to be invited back. For there *are* New Frontiers, exciting, promising, potentially sound, and not too far away. With some of the developing technologies, and a little luck, we may even be able to bypass a few of the methodological problems that ache for resolution now.

But I take a twilit view of this profession's future if we can't come to terms with the need for cooperatively financed research on methods. We live in a world of exploding technology, applied sciences based on widely shared conceptual and technical information. It could not have developed otherwise, proprietorship and patent laws notwithstanding.

We must retreat from attitudes of possessiveness in respect to research methods, and thereby free ourselves from the attendant limitations on adequate financing to do the long-overdue research on research.

Otherwise, in an era of nanosecond information retrieval and computation, world-wide electronic communications, leaps ahead in biology and medicine, and daring conquests in both space and time, we will have permitted advertising research to remain a cottage industry—not a dynamic New Frontier but a detached outpost—out of phase with almost all other areas of science and learning.

And, from where I stand, this stasis is both dangerous and unnecessary.

CHAPTER 6

Experimentation
in Advertising

by Seymour Banks

*Dr. Banks is vice president and manager of media and pro-
grams research, Leo Burnett Company, Inc. He also is a
lecturer in marketing at the University of Chicago and a
former associate professor of marketing at DePaul University.
He is on the editorial board of the* Journal of Marketing Research *and the author of* Experimentation in Marketing.

The type of experimentation in advertising I shall discuss is
quite pragmatic and utilitarian. It may yield only short-lived
information whose generalizability for other advertisers or for
the same advertiser at another time is moot. This comes about
because advertising deals with highly adaptive mechanisms,
to borrow the jargon of biology. In other words, advertising
research findings are a function of what both the experiment-
ing advertiser and his competition are doing at the time and
setting of the experiment.

This is not a gospel of despair but of reality. Even a short-
lived and small advantage may well be worth struggling to
achieve. Let us keep in mind that the process by which the
advertiser seeks to improve his efficiency is more important
than any particular finding.

As the foregoing paragraphs imply, I intend to confine my
remarks to advertising experimentation in real-life situations.

By real-life situations, I mean people being exposed to
advertising in standard commercial media contexts. This is in
opposition to laboratory settings such as theaters, trailers, or
workshops of various kinds in which advertising is exposed to
volunteers. I do not wish to denigrate laboratory experimenta-

tion because workers in this field have become extremely innovative in methodology, particularly in their use of behavioral rather than verbal responses. These advertising laboratories or workshops offer the advertising researcher many advantages, especially for copy testing.

Laboratory experimentation with its test universe of volunteers seems unsuitable, however, to those situations where attention is a key variable affecting response. Among these are intermedia or media mix comparisons and response to campaigns, particularly those of varying scheduling practices or of different expenditure levels. Nor does it permit measuring advertising's performance within the context of other parts of the marketing program.

ADVERTISING EXPERIMENT STATIONS

Probably the greatest challenge to advertising experimentation arises from the great variations in response to advertising from market to market resulting from variations in the advertiser's own sales levels, differences in competitive effort, and local natural or economic phenomena, to name only a few.

There are two traditional ways of coping with this problem. One is experimental design; for example, we can use a Latin-square design in which all treatments are rotated through each market. And this technique does have great value. For instance, the Department of Agriculture planned and executed a market test of three levels of advertising expenditure for fluid milk that met the stipulation that the research be able to detect a two per cent change in milk sales with 95 per cent confidence. For the cognoscenti, let me point out that they used an extra-period double-changeover design—using 6 markets arranged in two 3×3 Latin squares.

However, this experiment took two years to run and that's a very long time for today's marketing management. The other traditional technique is to use a large number of markets, allowing the beneficial effect of randomization to balance out these inter-market variations. But that costs money.

The new way to eliminate inter-market variations is through the development of what I wish to call "advertising experiment stations." I choose this name in honor of Professor Sandage who, with his usual prescience attempted 10 years ago to set up such a facility at the University of Illinois to serve advertisers in the same way agricultural experimental stations serve farmers. In the jargon of experimental design, these are split-plot designs that remove inter-market variations in performance from the data on response to experimental treatments by procedures that permit the use of several experimental treatments within each test market.

In contrast to the previous era in which each advertiser designed and administered his own experiment from start to finish, thus absorbing all costs, these new facilities have been developed and administered by an entrepreneur. Although the facilities are operated as a profit-making business, the individual advertiser gets the advantage of sharing costs with others. Such systems are available for both television and newspaper advertising.

First, I would like to describe the research facilities of these advertising experiment stations and then discuss some of the questions they are answering for advertisers.

CATV SYSTEMS

Two major techniques have been used for television experimentation. One type of installation uses CATV systems that have been specially wired so that different commercials can be shown simultaneously; the other system uses specially equipped TV receivers that will blank out commercials from one-half of a panel of homes upon command from the same antenna. In all cases, basic response data are collected from households rather than from stores. This is done because the homes receiving these different messages are distributed throughout a test-market area.

The development of CATV systems is so rapid that it is hard to keep up with them. But, as far as I can tell, there are four split-market CATV research systems in operation or being built: the oldest is Communications and Media Research Services, Inc., whose president recently received a patent for his split-cable technique; a second is AdTel, a private firm, which took over a project originally sponsored by the Advertising Research Foundation. In contrast to Communications and Media Research Services, which splits its Port Jervis, New York CATV system by neighborhoods, AdTel is wiring a new CATV market with two parallel cables so that they can have members of different panels living side-by-side on the same street, if desired.

The third system, TV Testing, was developed by a joint venture of a major market research company and the largest CATV operator in the country. In contrast with CMRS and AdTel, in which viewers are unaware that they are watching test commercials, under TV Testing's method, each home to be tested is called beforehand and asked to watch a specific show. Moreover, TV Testing does not use the simultaneous exposure pattern of the other two services. Instead, it uses a counter-balanced design in four markets: in market I, panel A sees a control commercial in week one; panel B sees the test commercial in week two. In market II, the sequence is reversed. This alternation is repeated in markets III and IV. In all cases, the commercials are placed in the same program.

CATV developers, almost by definition, are shrewd, aggressive men who are seeking to expand their return from their installations. As I was working on this paper, our agency received a letter from a CATV operator in upstate New York serving almost 7,000 subscribers in five communities. He asked us to consider the use of his system as an advertising laboratory. And he has the wherewithal: a system built in two loops so that a different commercial could be shown on each loop simultaneously, plus the necessary cameras, video tape, film chains, and time clocks to allow insertion of test and control commercials in specified program contexts. So he's No. 4.

No doubt, as CATV systems grow in size and as developers and owners grow in sophistication, more and more CATV facilities will be available for advertising experiments.

MILWAUKEE ADVERTISING LABORATORY

The other major television technique is one developed by the Milwaukee Journal Company to serve as the Milwaukee

Advertising Laboratory. This has a very elaborate methodology because it uses normal through-the-air television transmission rather than cable. Two test panels, located within the Milwaukee TV area, are equipped with special circuitry on their television sets so that, when an appropriate signal is telecast from a station's antenna, one panel receives a test commercial in the normal fashion while the sets in the other panel go dark and mute. Since another commercial cannot be substituted for the one on the air, tests involving two strategies require that both be telecast, one being blanked out for panel A and the other blanked out for panel B.

Newspapers have long offered advertisers split-run facilities, which permit simultaneous usage of differing treatments. However, that entire system rested upon mail inquiries or mail-order purchases. It was not applicable to the usual kind of national advertising that is designed to motivate purchases in stores, nor could it be used to evaluate campaigns.

However, newspaper versions of the CATV system have been set up by some newspapers who have achieved two basic requirements: very high coverage of their markets, and circulation that is almost completely home-delivered. Without pretending to complete reporting of this type of facility, let me point out that the Milwaukee Journal Company and the Des Moines Register and Tribune have developed a system whereby split-runs can be sorted by carrier routes. Therefore, it is possible to identify those areas that received specific advertisements and to develop control over exposure to newspaper campaigns in the same fashion as is used for television. Thus, the Milwaukee Advertising Laboratory actually offers an advertiser the opportunity to test newspaper and TV mixes.

The logical conclusion of this movement toward advertising experiment stations has been drawn by Market Facts. They have set up a Marketest Division, which acts as a wholesaler in four medium-sized markets—Erie, Dayton, Wichita, and Fresno. By use of their own warehouses and trucks, and frequent visits to stores, they eliminate out-of-stock conditions and maintain consistent shelf conditions in order to eliminate these variables from the data.

Newspapers in these markets split their press runs on a four-way basis corresponding to four marketing zones, which are matched on the basis of store volume, chain composition, and store customer characteristics. PAR and other firms have also developed these controlled test markets.

So much for hardware.

What kinds of problems have these advertising experiment stations been used for?

1. *Tests of advertising expenditures.* One advertiser tried doubling his brand's budget while another tried cutting his budget in half. Because dollar values for the advertising costs and incremental gains (or losses) of sales were easily available, it was possible to show that the extra spending was profitable whereas the cut in advertising reduced sales so much that the net effect was a reduction in profits.

   In a third test, a new brand was introduced at two different levels of advertising expenditures—one corresponding to a national expenditure of $1,150,000 for a 20-week period, the other to a rate of $1,750,000. Although the additional advertising produced additional sales, the higher advertising level was not viable. Again, on a national scale, the additional $600,000 of advertising generated an estimated one million dollars of sales—an advertising-to-sales ratio of 60 per cent.

2. *Tests of media scheduling practices.* The winning scheduling procedure generated one-half its extra buyers from users of the test brand's competitors and one-half from people who had not used any of this type of product in the previous 24 weeks and might be considered as new users.

3. *Tests to determine whether it is better for an advertiser using network TV for his basic effort to use spot TV or newspapers for supplementary advertising.* Since one of our clients is involved in this study, all I can say is that we are studying these results with a great deal of interest.

Now let's discuss some other types of projects that might be studied, particularly on CATV systems where it is possible to make modifications in the program structure itself as well as move commercials from program to program.

4. *Studies of program context and commercial placement.* One could study the influence of program content or style on commercial performance, e.g., do commercials for a food product do as well in a hard-hitting action program oriented to men as in a situation comedy?

Viewers often complain about commercials interrupting a program, but advertisers fear to cluster their commercials for fear of loss of response. By using a given program in two forms, one with commercials as they are now used and a second in which all commercials are grouped in a single block, one might find out two things: (1) will reducing commercial interruptions improve viewer ratings? (2) will commercial performance weaken and, if so, who will suffer most—the first advertiser in a cluster, the middle one, or the last?

5. *Studies of commercial wear-out.* It would be possible to continue to run the same pool of commercials on one split-half of the system for a year or so while trying new pools periodically on the other half to see whether the phenomenon of wear-out really exists and, if so, when it sets in.

PARA-EXPERIMENTS

Let me close by stating that I have a substantial regard for experimentation's role in helping us be more certain about causality in a complicated and uncontrollable world. Experimentation is not, however, the only way to generate understanding.

I suggest that we can use lessons we have learned from experimentation to help us learn more from day-to-day operations and accidental variations in effort. Let's call these "para-experiments."

First of all, a word or two about our old and somewhat passé friend—test marketing. No controls, no experiment design. On the other hand, when market tests are carefully run, you can learn a great deal.

One of the great virtues of test marketing is that it functions like insurance—it may cost you some money but it protects you against a very big loss.

Everybody talks about successes. Let me tell you about a failure that was spotted early by a well-run test market operation. This kept one of our clients from losing a million dollars.

Upon the basis of eight months of test marketing a new product, we estimated national projected sales of over 300,000 cases, a volume that would have generated a total amount for advertising, promotion, and profit of $700,000. But it would have cost $1,800,000 for advertising and promotion. When you spend $1,800,000 for advertising and promotion and get back $700,000, you have a loss of $1,100,000.

Assuming that advertising and promotion could be cut back to zero and sales continued as they had the last 4 months of the 8-month test market operation, the net loss at the end of Year 1 would have dropped to $900,000. On the other hand, going on at full blast for a full year would have produced a loss of more than one and a half million dollars. Thus a relatively low-cost test market operation saved not only a million dollars but also manpower and time.

Finally, let's turn our attention to the oldest of research procedures—sales analysis. Our newest genie—the computer—can help us out in a way that brings sparkle to this previously humdrum effort.

First of all, we must accept the idea that, in order to gain the greatest control over the advertising process, we must obtain both input and output data from geographical areas that have operational definitions. By that, I refer to areas in which advertising can be adjusted to any degree desired from full blast on to off. For most major advertisers in the packaged goods fields, these operationally defined areas are television markets, since they also provide radio, newspaper, and outdoor media plus—in some of the largest markets—spot magazines.

Therefore, we must find means of converting our own accounting systems based upon invoices into market research systems keyed to small geographic areas. This is terribly difficult but the new technologies of telecommunication of sales data, machine readable-record systems, and the computer all help.

I think we will also get help from the outside since it now looks like computers and recent developments in retailing will make good-quality market research data available from wholesaler withdrawal records at relatively low costs. This movement has started in the food industry and will probably spread. Several firms are now in the business of reworking computer tapes from chain food warehouses and wholesalers and reporting the results on a market-by-market basis. Because goods are now priced at retail when shipped, and because practically no inventory is kept at stores, these shipment data are quite close to actual retail sales.

As time goes on and more and more business record-keeping systems are computerized, the old barriers to information transmittal that required the creation of market research may erode and crumble away. Thus, good data may become available much more readily and less expensively than they do now. Consequently, better data for smaller and more operationally significant areas will become available. How can we interpret them?

One of the great virtues of experiments is that we get into the habit of keeping very good records of everything that goes on. The same habit must be developed for para-experiments, keeping records of exactly what we did, market-by-market, plus what our competition and Nature are doing so we can take those facts into consideration in our analysis. Once more, the computer comes to our rescue, making analyses of multiple covariance feasible. This technique enables us to adjust our own data for variations in effort by others.

Experimentation uses experimental design to compensate for variations in known factors that affect sales, like region, city size, brand share, etc. In para-experiments, we can substitute classification schemes for experimental design, analyzing our data on a cell-by-cell basis rather than on an aggregate basis.

Finally, since our treatments on para-experiments were not randomly distributed to markets but were deliberately or accidentally allocated, we must be skeptical about any single finding that a given strategy seems to be associated with a gain or loss in sales. We must insist on seeing this pattern repeated several times before we believe it.

The essence of control and causality is repetition. Experimentation must meet this test as well as para-experimentation, although we probably will ask for fewer repetitions of effect from experiments than from para-experiments.

To sum up, let me state that we can gain a great deal from experimentation by applying its fundamental concepts and analytical apparatus to ordinary non-experimental data. In doing so, we must act with caution and conservatism, accepting the hypothesis that a given treatment has produced a given result only after we have sought and rejected all other explanations and only after we have found the same consequence occurring repetitively.

BIBLIOGRAPHY

Brown, George H. "Measuring the Sales Effectiveness of Alternative Media," *Proceedings of the 7th Annual Conference of the Advertising Research Foundation,* October, 1961.

Becknell, James C., Jr. "Use of Experimental Design in the Study of Media Effectiveness," *Media/Scope,* August, 1962, pp. 46–49.

Becknell, James C., Jr., and Robert W. McIsaac, "Test Marketing Cookware Coated with 'Teflon,'" *Journal of Advertising Research,* 3, 3 (September, 1963), 2–8.

Clement, Wendell E., Peter L. Henderson, Cleveland P. Ely, "The Effect of Different Levels of Promotional Expenditures on Sales of Fluid Milk," USDA Economic Research Service ERS-259, October, 1965.

Hardin, David K., "A New Approach to Test Marketing," *Journal of Marketing,* 30 (October, 1966), 28–31.

Henderson, Peter L., James F. Hind, and Sidney E. Brown, "Sales Effects of Two Campaign Themes," *Journal of Advertising Research,* I, 6 (December, 1961), 2–11.

Stewart, John P., *Repetitive Advertising in Newspapers* (Boston: Harvard University, Division of Research, Graduate School of Business Administration, 1964).

——— "CATV: Panacea for Ad Testing," *Television Age,* April 22, 1968, pp. 26 ff.

CHAPTER 7

Survey Approaches in Advertising

by A. Edward Miller

Mr. Miller is president of the Berlitz Schools of Languages. He was formerly president of The World Publishing Company, president of Alfred Politz Research Company, publisher of McCall's and a vice president and director of the McCall Corporation, and assistant to the publisher, Time, Inc. He also has taught at the Baruch School of Business, City University of New York, and in the Business School of New York University.

As I started to think about what I might discuss with you, it occurred to me that to a greater degree than most marketing people I have had the opportunity to view marketing and advertising research from a number of different perspectives. I started in research for *Life* magazine. I took leave of research to become publisher of *McCall's*, where I was very much concerned with the results of advertising and media and marketing research studies because they were a significant factor in my ultimate success or failure as a publisher. From there to Alfred Politz for four years of professional research experience. Now I speak from the point of view of a man running a book publishing and printing enterprise. Ironically the book business has never utilized research in a meaningful way but I believe it will.

Whatever I say is tempered by the fact that as a businessman, as a research director, as a so-called "professional researcher," I have been directly responsible for or had an influence upon over a hundred million dollars of research. All of that experience has put me in my advanced years in a position where my prejudices have become my considered judgments.

SOME QUESTIONS ABOUT RESEARCH

Summing up my experience leads me to talk with you not in terms of dogma and assertions but in regard to some areas of honest confusion that have resulted from these experiences. My confusion is not confined to advertising research alone—I share these questions about research in the total spectrum of marketing research.

First, I am confused as to why research has failed to live up to the challenge of the needs of American business. In this question is the suggestion that I believe research has failed to make significant progress in coping with the problems of business. This I do indeed believe. I believe it is more true of advertising research than it is true of marketing research, because it is more difficult to set objectives for advertising accomplishment than it is to set marketing objectives. I think that the basic reason for lack of progress in research is inadequate communications between management and research. Management still does not feel comfortable in dealing with the technical, decimal-point world of the researcher. The researcher, on the other hand, does not feel comfortable in the risk-taking, decision-making, policy-setting world of management. I am confused about why they have so rarely sat down together to talk things out in order to reach understanding. I think there is a great opportunity for this dialogue to happen on some college campus around the country if ever things settle down a bit.

That is a basic confusion. I have many more. I am confused by the lack of real technical progress in research. The technology of research today is not very significantly different from what it was twenty years ago. If you want to argue that one, compare the progress in marketing or advertising research with the progress made in the study of physics or chemistry or biophysics or any of the physical sciences. Compare the research progress we have made with the progress made in the total world of communications during the last twenty years. Advertising research pales in this comparison.

As we study the elements that comprise technical progress, I am again confused. Why has there been such limited progress in sampling technology in the twenty years since the revolution in which the principles of science and probability were applied to sampling for marketing and advertising research?

The substantial lack of progress in developing the skills of questioning confuses me. It is still much more an art than a science. Principles of question-asking that enable us to generalize have developed very little. To a significant degree we are still utilizing the unique experience of an individual researcher or a given research company.

I am confused by the limited progress we have made in handling the very pragmatic problems of the people who are our interviewers. There is little progress in interviewer training or in some coordinated effort to weed out the ineffective or dishonest interviewers.

I am confused about why the research business has been so slow to learn the difference between measuring the *opinions* and *attitudes* of consumers and the *behavior* of the consumer. I am even more puzzled about why there has been so little progress in learning of the great insights provided by interrelating consumer opinions and consumer behavior.

Every once in a while in my confused state I reach out for the view from another planet. In one make-believe conversation I envisioned what one of the greatest *obfuscators* of them all— Marshall McLuhan—might say about the business of marketing research. I have a hunch he might be hostile to the very notion of research because some of his more glorious concepts might be inhibited or denied by research. While I am sure he would not be slowed down, he would inevitably raise the question of whether or not the masses of people innovate or create. He would talk about the great limitations in our communications between question-asker and question-answerer. He would point out that our research communications are bound by the written word. Even though we use the spoken word to elicit response we are bound by the hastily written word. We miss the inflection of the voice. We miss the satirical twist of inflection. We miss the intensity of emotion. We miss the smile, the raised eyebrow, and the innuendo. Basically we miss all non-verbal communications which may represent a majority of all communications. Mr. McLuhan might just be right. I am confused because I find myself understanding and agreeing with the McLuhan I have conjured up.

I am confused about the use of the computer in marketing and advertising research. The computer has revolutionized the cost of handling data, the speed of handling data, the quantities of data that may be handled, and finally and possibly most important, the kind of analyses that may be made. Unfortunately, there are few business or advertising men capable of dealing with this kind of advanced analysis, so, by and large, we are not farming nearly as well as we now know how to farm. One very good researcher expressed it neatly when in answer to criticism he said, "It's not very smart for a researcher to show up the limitations and incompetence of his management is it?" I'm not sure.

WHERE THE RESPONSIBILITY LIES

I'm confused about where to put the responsibility for the all-too-slow progress we have been making in research. The responsibility must be *shared* by the research fraternity and by management. In approaching this kind of soul-searching, I am reminded of a remark that Harry Truman made when he was accused of being particularly nasty to some group. He simply said, "I never give them hell. I just tell the truth and they think it is hell." Let's try to tell the truth. A lot of what has developed is the responsibility of the research director. Management basically wants help from research in making marketing and advertising decisions.

Business spends over $16 billion dollars a year to *talk* to the consumer by way of advertising. Business spends only about $500 million dollars a year to *listen* to the consumer by way of research. There is quite a gap between the money spent to communicate to the consumer and the money spent to listen to him. This is a real communications gap.

The amount of money spent to finance research is *one* of the factors in the limited usefulness of research to marketing management. Many research directors believe that one of their important tasks is to get research at the lowest possible cost. The auction-sale type of research results. The lowest bidder gets the research job.

I was in an airplane last week when we were having rough weather. The man next to me leaned over and said, "Did you ever stop to think that every part of this plane we're in was bought on the basis of a low bid?" Makes one stop and think.

Many other forces and factors are at work. Money or budget is really one of the less significant factors—it is more likely a symptom than a cause. The cause is the attitude of researchers who tend to consider themselves fact-finders and not problem-solvers. The decimal-point–oriented researcher does not effectively communicate to management. Management, on the other hand, has been remiss in not acquiring sufficient knowledge to fully comprehend the researcher and in failing to set up management objectives that lend themselves to research measurement.

Just last week the research head of a large marketing research company came in to see me to talk about a research study in the world of books. I was interested in the company because of their previous experience in the field. At the end of our talk I said, "Of course, your report will include your suggestions and recommendations for marketing and advertising action based on your research and your experience." His answer was, "No, we don't make recommendations. We have been successful because we confine ourselves to reporting the factual data we develop." We parted company, probably never to meet again. Am I right in expecting suggestions for management action from research?

SOME QUESTIONS ABOUT ADVERTISING RESEARCH

My confusion is even more intense in the more specific area of advertising research. I am confused by the fact that although tens or possibly hundreds of millions of dollars have been spent in copy research, very few general principles or concepts of advertising copy have evolved. There is no philosophy of advertising copy. There are some schools of copy approach based on some empirical experiences with little or no meaning for the next piece of copy to be written.

Many large companies have become disenchanted with the endless trials involved in continually testing and revising and retesting ads and have settled for crude testing salted down with liberal doses of good judgment.

Similar observations can be made about media testing. Here again we have large and conspicuous voids in our knowledge, and I am confused by the whole approach. I see a number of services producing large quantities of data on a regular basis. Many of these services are overlapping; they are measuring essentially the same thing. Economic pressures force them to use small samples and in some instances crude questioning techniques. I am confused about why there has been no effort to coordinate and standardize measurements so that advertisers and agencies get a maximum of data for the dollars they invest in this kind of research. I see definitions of reading or audiences that are not advertiser-oriented. I see studies put on a regular cycle basis for the benefit of the research and not the medium or the researchers evaluating the media.

I am confused by the absence of advertising research that shows the differing effects of the various advertising media. I believe there are copy overtones that affect the ultimate success of the given ad. In other words, I believe there is an interaction between copy and advertising medium. I am confused because most research has not reflected or measured this rather basic hypothesis.

I am confused because there is very little research on the differing effects of different media on a given piece of copy. There is at least one significant study that shows that an identical ad placed in different magazine environments could have a variation in effect of a factor or two or three. Despite these startling figures, I see very little being done to develop this research. It seems to me that this should be a rather basic area of concern for advertisers.

I am confused when I observe advertising agencies all going

through essentially the same primitive ritual in using the computer to make better media decisions. I see no constructive efforts on the part of advertising agencies to pull together to have joint computer activities in this area of media evaluation. It could save everyone considerable sums of money if we could achieve reasonable standardization of the input data to evaluate media. It could produce better information for better decisions at lower cost.

I am confused by the lack of progress in the application of scientific method to the study of advertising and marketing in contrast with some of the harder sciences. Some lessons may be learned by viewing the pattern for their success. Let's look at medicine for a comparison. What is the source of research development in the medical sciences? Very little of total medical research comes from the drug companies or from the companies that make medical supplies. Obviously, doctors as individual practitioners do not perform any significant proportion of research. Research is sponsored by government agencies and by universities and university-connected hospitals. Medicine has had a dramatic and successful pattern of progress in operating in this fashion.

What is the advertising research equivalent of medical research? Individual practitioners of advertising research do not have the resources or margins needed to indulge in much basic research. Some individual advertisers do a little bit of research but what they do is essentially kept very secret and private. Unless they are shared by a large number of advertisers, these studies won't help very much. There are a few groups like the Advertising Research Foundation and the Marketing Science Institute, which have some potential for a broad-spectrum research approach to advertising research. To date, these groups have not had the common support and resources to make a significant contribution to solving some of the more fundamental problems of advertising. It is problematic whether they will indeed achieve the level of support it will take to undertake meaningful and basic research.

How then do we get to the development of basic research on advertising? Although there have been isolated projects of considerable interest, there is no pattern of broad-based research in advertising going on at present in the universities. If this research is indeed in progress, then the schools have done a poor job of communicating what they are doing. I was impressed recently by the research that Columbia University had announced in an effort to understand the behavior of the consumer in the market place. (I believe that the focus of this research should now be changed to try to understand the behavior of Columbia University students on campus.) I believe the universities must assume leadership in research on advertising if we are to achieve real progress in this area.

When the universities enter the field in strength, I hope we can get away from the customary study of detailed and isolated elements and deal instead in terms of basic research. I am confused by the fact that researchers seem to pay very little attention to research on the brain and the mind and memory. Such studies have most important long-range significance for advertising. We must learn more about how the mind works. I think we must probe the mysteries of memory. What is retained? How is it stored? Why is it retained? We really have very little understanding of the mind and memory.

GOVERNMENT AND RESEARCH

I am confused by the role of government in marketing and advertising research. The Department of Commerce spends so little for marketing and advertising research that it is almost embarrassing to report it. As a matter of fact, I am concerned about the total governmental attitude toward research.

Some time ago I took the time to talk with Esther Peterson about her work as White House adviser on consumer affairs. She was honest enough to tell me that her work on consumer attitudes and behavior was predicated basically on complaints. We all know, just as Esther Peterson knew, that complaints do not provide a sound basis for enacting legislation to affect business and the consumer. There is sufficient know-how available in marketing and advertising research to be able to go to a cross section of the consuming public and to ascertain their attitudes and their behavior in relation to given areas of sensitivity in the consumer buying area.

I recently heard one of the top people in the Health, Education, and Welfare Department tell an audience that unless they told the government their attitudes about insurance they might see some legislation enacted that they might not like. I think it is unrealistic to expect that kind of response. If the government wants to know what people want in insurance, they can ask them by means of marketing research.

I proposed to both Mrs. Peterson and her successor, Betty Furness, that a study be undertaken for the continuing measurement of consumer buying satisfaction with 100 products and services. The result would be reported to businessmen and to government on a completely objective basis. This research, it is hoped, would enable business to discipline itself in terms of consumer abuses or shortcomings before there was a need to enact legislation. In the event that business did not correct itself over a period of time, the continuing index would point a finger at deficiencies in business's capacity for self-discipline and legislation might then be needed. In any event, I believe we would benefit from specific tangible measurements of what the consumer experiences and what the consumer thinks about the products and services he or she buys. That program is still being considered, but it is not very likely that it will materialize since everyone seems to be somewhat nervous about the prospect of having complete and adequate information in this area.

Another area of potentially useful application of advertising and marketing research skills may be in providing congressmen and senators with a continuing measurement of the opinions of their constituency. As you know, when the Constitution of this country was created, a congressional district was conceived to be the area a man could cover in a day on horseback. Somebody way back then was thinking about meaningful communication between legislators and their constituency. Today, with all the improvements available to us in the form of modern communications we probably experience fewer and less meaningful communications than ever before.

I propose that the art or science of consumer research be made available to each of our legislators four times a year for a true sampling of their districts to find out what their constituents think about issues of the day. One portion of these questions would be standard, the same for all legislators, and another portion could be devoted to questions of local or regional interest. Although congressmen and senators do not simply reflect the views of their constituents, it seems to me that it would be very helpful to have those views known as one element of the complex decision-making process in which our legislators are constantly engaged.

These are only two indications of the infinite number of further applications that exist for marketing and advertising research. Perhaps the riots and the rebellions we are experiencing might be understood, and conceivably might have been prevented, if we had had the benefit of a continuing dialogue with a particular group by way of research.

TEMPERING SCIENCE WITH HUMAN VALUES

Although I have tried to make a plea for science in our scheme of things, I have some confused emotions on this score. I think one of the most significant factors in our society is the sense of values each of us establishes in his or her pattern of living. Research has not made a meaningful penetration into that important personal world. I think we need a perspective on the role of science in our way of life. Let me read you one written by a man for whom I have great respect, Milton Eisenhower, President of Johns Hopkins University. In an article entitled "Only Game Fish Swim Upstream," Dr. Eisenhower said:

> We are building a strange and complex world, complete with masers and lasers, transistors, and tranquilizers, radar and radioactivity. We have computers and cobalt bombs and freeze-dried foods and satellites and baby dolls that talk. One day, we will unravel the secret of the genes, solve the riddle of photosynthesis, harness the sun's energy, triumph over disease, and populate space.
>
> This is quite a different world from the one I knew as a boy. Then there was not a single industrial research laboratory in the

country. The automobile seemed a humorous display of apparent futility. And doctors relied more on the power of suggestion than on medicine.

But now we come ever closer to the great golden age that has eluded men since Adam. I think man has the ability to build this new world, but I am concerned about his ability to live in it.

I would wager that man will conquer the solar system before he conquers hate. He will harness the sun before he harnesses his baser emotions. Modern man worships at the temple of science, but science tells him only what is possible, not what is right. To know that, we must develop a perspective on the human condition; we must study and esteem man, not simply in the composite but as an individual. Birth rates, death rates, crime rates, consumer surveys, polls, medians, means, and averages—all of these notwithstanding, human experience cannot be reduced to numbers and formulae. Man is not born and does not die collectively. He enters this world as he leaves it—alone.

We need a new breed of human beings to populate the world we are building—people who are humanists in the broadest sense, with an awareness of their heritage, a faith in the cardinal spiritual concepts which gave birth to human freedom, and an acceptance of man's responsibilities to his fellow man. We truly need a NEW breed of human beings. And, I do believe that the college students of today, rather than being merely "restless" or "rootless," may be the first generation of New Americans—compassionate, courageous, committed, and involved.

Milton Eisenhower said it well. Research is not just a simple collection of fact. I believe it is an integral part of our way of life. It should have a meaningful role in science, in industry, in government, in education, in marketing and advertising, and every basic human activity.

However, science must be tempered by human judgment and taste. The problems of advertising today are caused by people who have abused the privilege of talking to the many by means of advertising. They have not troubled themselves to listen to the reaction from the many to whom they have addressed their messages.

If you want some perspective on advertising, talk to some young people, not in formal research but in informal conversations. I think you will find just as I have found that the hyperbole that seems so essential to advertising today does not set well. They are critical of those ads that are deserving of criticism. I have heard Harry Dolan, the well-known writer who happens to be a Negro, talk about television and other advertising as seen through the perspective of a Negro family. It makes you cringe to get his view of what is being said and done in the name of advertising.

The simplest kind of research can point up these important qualities of advertising so often missed—elements of good taste, truthfulness, meaningful communications. This is not a research problem, but it is an area in which research can help us to bring a greater measure of integrity and confidence to advertising.

CHAPTER 8

Psychological Approaches in Advertising Research

by Burleigh B. Gardner

Dr. Gardner is the founder and president of Social Research, Inc. He has been engaged in teaching and research at the University of Chicago, where he was associated with Professor W. Lloyd Warner in social and economic studies. He co-authored Deep South *and* Human Relations in Industry.

Before talking about advertising research, I want to talk about advertising as a problem in communications. Every advertiser is using these communications in an effort to influence people. The most vociferous critics of advertising are also trying through communications (i.e., speeches, articles, and books) to influence people. Thus, the advertiser is one part of the vast array of would-be influencers trying to reach the minds and influence the behavior of men.

Now the goal of advertising (like the goal of a candidate's political speech) is action. The advertiser wants the audience to buy his product; the candidate wants its vote. The two ends of the process are clear—reception of the message and later action at the supermarket or polling booth. However, between these ends lies a complex and little understood process—the *terra incognita* of the human mind. Thus, any communication that is meaningful involves psychological processes within the mind of the listener.

Many an advertiser and researcher tries to evade the complexity of the issue by saying, "I don't care about the process, just tell me if my ads will sell my product." This pragmatic approach is most readily applied to personal selling—the good salesman brings in the orders. However, there is also considerable interest in knowing *how* the good salesman does it. In fact, most of the research on personal selling is directed to understanding the selling process in order to be able to train salesmen in the right way to do it.

For practical purposes, much advertising research today is directed toward predicting future behavior. "Will this ad or campaign create desire for the product and therefore lead to sales?" This means that the research must attend to the intermediate process in the mind that takes place between ad exposure and product purchase. It must probe the mind in such a way as to give some basis for prediction.

There has been some controversy among people engaged in advertising research as to whether changes in "attitude" or "image" precede changes in buying behavior. Some have claimed they could find no evidence that such changes occurred. The implication of their argument is that the advertising message directly affects later buying behavior without having any influence on the mind. This clearly doesn't make sense. Somehow the influence of the communication must have changed the psychological set, or else nothing different would happen.

Clearly these researchers have equated their inability to measure the changes in psychological state with absence of changes. They say in effect, "Since I couldn't measure it, it wasn't there." When one examines both their conceptual approach and their methodology (at least what appears in print), it is clear that both were inadequate.

In contrast, other researchers have been demonstrating that changes in the state of mind do anticipate changes in buying behavior. With mass market items, they find that certain shifts in a brand image will increase the probability that the brand will be purchased. This has been demonstrated in the market place and not in contrived experiments or under controlled conditions. Thus, in the normal operations of the market place, with competition operating both in advertising and at point of sale, these researchers have shown that changes in the set of mind toward a brand are related to actual behavior.

HOW ADVERTISING WORKS

At present, we can state a general theory of how advertising works as follows: Every person has a body of knowledge, attitudes, and feelings with respect to different brands of a product. These may be vague and not very articulate, or they may be very strong and clear. They make up what we call an "image" of the brand, which is a set of mind and predisposition with respect to it. Where the "image" is favorable and makes the product seem appropriate to the individual, he will tend to buy it. If his attitude toward it is strongly favorable, he will be very brand-loyal.

When he receives an advertising message for a brand, it somehow becomes integrated into his previous set of mind. In some cases, it may significantly alter the previous set; in others, it will make little change. Unless there is change, we can expect no change in the way he will act toward the brand.

However, this set of mind seems to be quite stable and does not change rapidly or drastically under the impact of a single message. Experience has shown that repetition of ads is necessary before much change results. Some measurements are beginning to show how many messages are needed before measurable changes take place.

Repetitive advertising does not necessarily change the brand image but causes an increase in the brand awareness. Apparently, the brand images are not deeply buried in the unconscious, but are in the pre-conscious level of the mind. With any stimulation or clues, they can move up to the conscious level. Under the stimulation of repetitive advertising, the brand and its associations seem to be closer to consciousness and more easily recalled.

THE TOOLS OF ADVERTISING RESEARCH

All this is extremely relevant to advertising research, since advertising is an effort to change this set of mind, this predisposition toward the brand or product or company. And advertising research is directed toward the practical ends of guiding this effort or evaluating its results.

In this research, we have a limited array of tools and methods. A few are instruments that rely on measures of physiological reactions upon exposure to an advertisement. The common ones are the polygraph to measure changes in pulse, blood pressure, breathing, or perspiration; the eye camera to measure pupil dilation or to measure eye movement. They measure actual changes, but the problem lies in determining the relevance of the changes to assessing advertising. Thus, what does pupil dilation tell us about the changes in the set of mind induced by the ad?

The principal tools in use rely on communications. We ask questions, administer tests, stimulate conversation, all to the end of determining the relevant set of mind. Thus, we probe the mind through communications in an attempt to determine the set that will influence future behavior. Thus, we ask directly or indirectly how the respondent will vote or how he feels about candidates. We ask him to make comparative ratings or semantic differentials. We ask him to explain his feelings or his choices. From this verbal behavior, we then try to deduce how he will vote or what communications will induce him to change.

In discussing psychological approaches, it is common to think in terms of special techniques of collecting data. It is also often believed that the "psychological approach" requires somewhat esoteric data. Thus, response to a TAT (Thematic Apperception Test) picture is believed to yield psychological data while answers to direct questions do not. And this school of thought holds that the researcher using projective techniques is doing psychological research, even though he reduces the responses to simple statistics, which could have been obtained with a simple structured questionnaire.

The Psychological Approach

Actually, a "psychological approach" is dependent upon the knowledge and skill the researcher brings to bear on the interpretation of data. If he is well trained in psychology, he brings to bear theories and knowledge that enable him to draw conclusions that may differ from those drawn by someone with a M.B.A. degree. *It is not the data they work from, but what they see in it that makes the difference.*

In planning a study to guide the advertiser, there are a number of questions the psychologist may raise:

1. How does the product fit into the style of life of the user?
2. What are the non-rational meanings and associations of the product and how do they relate to the product usage?
3. Are there personality patterns specially relevant to the product usage and meanings?
4. What meanings should be communicated to attract users?
5. What are the relevant target groups to which communication can be addressed?
6. What are the symbols most appropriate or least appropriate for this purpose?

These questions can be applied whether the problem is one of a new or old product, a brand, or a corporation. They can be applied to a single communication, a campaign theme, or a total campaign. They can be applied to research to help generate creative approaches or to studies to evaluate alternate advertising concepts or actual ads.

Let me illustrate with a description of a specific problem:

A cigarette manufacturer was trying to aim brands at very specific market segments, such as working men, young lower middle-class women, etc. He wanted guidance in designing packages that would express an image that would appeal to each market segment.

From past experience, we knew that the semantic differential would be an effective and efficient technique to explore subtle reactions to form and color as used in package design. A study was designed to test reactions to basic elements of form and a range of colors.

Analysis of this data provided a basic handbook on reactions to form and color. This handbook was then used by designers to produce packages that would express the desired images.

Application of Psychological Data

Research can be directed toward helping create effective ads or toward evaluating ads after the creative effort. Unfortunately, most effort goes into evaluating ads after they are prepared and, as might be expected, the creative people are usually hostile to this effort. They feel, and not entirely without cause, that the research hampers new concepts or approaches.

Ideally, research should help create effective advertising and not merely be limited to evaluating advertising after the fact. This means guidance for the creative people in deciding what to say and how to say it. This can involve exploration of the constellation of meanings and feelings that surround a product, to find the needs (both conscious and practical and unconscious) it should serve.

This involves a kind of research and analysis that should go far beyond the ordinary simple listings of "reasons why" or characteristics of the "ideal product." This may lead to descriptions of personality patterns that are relevant to the problem. This may further lead to concepts of market segments based on socio-psychological classifications.

For example, in studies of laxatives it was found that upper middle-class people wanted a laxative with gentle action but working-class people wanted a laxative with powerful action. It was clear that in reaching the working-class market the advertiser should communicate strong, positive action, and all the symbolism in ads or package should convey this. This clearly indicated the use of colors, forms in package and label design, layout design for print ads, etc.

Another study was concerned with the associations with the concept "flame." One approach used was to ask people to imagine "flame" as a person and to describe him or her. This showed the following:

"Flame" stimulates intense emotional responses. It evokes rich fantasies of people who are dramatic, sensuous, and outgoing.

"Flame" is not well controlled, is impetuous, dangerous, given to moods and outbursts, probably a redhead.

In addition, "flame" evokes ideas of sensory gratifications (often oral), and enveloping warmth and security.

Studies of this type can help creative people understand the subtleties of associations and the evocative responses to concepts and symbols they may use. Well-done research of this type can thus help sharpen the communicative skill of the artist and copywriter.

These studies rely on considerable probing of the set of mind of the respondents. While everyone has somewhat different patterns of associations, there are usually a few predominant clusters, which appear again and again. In fact, unless there were such general patterns, communication would be impossible because each person would interpret a symbol or set of symbols differently.

Conversational or "depth" interviews are very useful for discerning significant patterns. When properly designed, such interviews can reveal much about the individual's personality, style of life, and personal goals, as well as his attitudes toward brands or products. This gives the analyst a rich body of information from which to make his interpretations.

The various projective techniques can elicit similar rich materials. However, they, too, rely on the skill and experience of the analyst for providing sound understanding.

For some problems, more restricted techniques are needed. For example, if you want to measure small differences in reaction, a semantic differential is often more sensitive than many other techniques. It is sensitive enough to show the differences in reactions to different colors or even different shades of one color.

When using the semantic differential or other rating scales, it is possible to use computer technology for large samples. With a properly designed semantic differential, it is possible to classify individuals on certain personality patterns and then relate their reactions to ads to these classifications. For example, in a recent study, we used a questionnaire combining semantic differentials with open-end questions. Analysis of the interviews started with a factor analysis of the S.D. ratings that gave four principal factors. Each respondent was then scored for his factor weights and these were correlated with all other variables to show the important relationships. In interpreting the open-end material, we grouped responses for people high on separate factor scores. Thus, people high on a "status" factor were examined as a group, those high on "impulsivity" as another, and so on. The final analysis of the open-end material showed how the different groups reacted to different ads and advertising appeals.

There is often a desire to use personality traits as a way of classifying consumers. In some studies, attempts have been made to use standard personality tests as a basis for such classifications. In general, these attempts have proven little about buying behavior or response to advertising. The problem lies primarily in the fact that these tests were developed for other purposes and the classifications are not relevant for advertising purposes. Such tests will not identify the "innovator" who will respond to a new product, or the "status seeker," or other types or traits that may be relevant to the advertiser.

As a result, the researcher concerned with personality traits must develop techniques appropriate to his purpose. And before that he needs to conceptualize what traits may be relevant. For example, in studies of public attitudes toward big corporations, we found through open-end interviews many people who had a generally negative attitude toward big business. These negative attitudes seemed to color their reactions to companies and to their advertising. In order to measure this general negativism, we developed a series of questions that would place people on a scale from extremely favorable to extremely negative. We validated this on large samples and found a high correlation between scores on the scale and attitudes toward specific companies.

Finally, I want to emphasize that to understand the processes in the mind and to relate them to advertising requires much more research effort than has so far been applied. Furthermore, it is research that will require application of psychological concepts and methods in the hands of well-trained professionals. This is a field where we need more in the way of insight and understanding than new techniques or methodology.

And even at the present stage, we need to learn more about how advertising research can be made more useful to the creators of advertising. The gap between research and creative people is far too great, and until it is bridged, research will do little to shape advertising communication.

CHAPTER 9

Computer Applications to Advertising Decisions

by Peter Langhoff

Dr. Langhoff is president of American Research Bureau, Inc., a subsidiary of Control Data Corporation. He formerly was a senior vice president of Young and Rubicam. He also has served as a consultant to the U.S. Department of Defense and the Hoover Commission, and was employed by the Veterans Administration, Federal Works Agency, Rural Electrification Administration, and National Resources Board. Books he has edited and contributed to include Models, Measurement, and Marketing *and* Criteria for Marketing and Advertising Research.

The computer frontier in advertising was penetrated in the middle 1950's. What lay beyond this frontier was little known but wide open to imaginative, if unbounded, speculation. Today the electronic computer is making a substantial contribution to advertising, though not in the manner some had expected and hoped for. Certainly with the advantage of more than ten years' experience, we are now in a better position to gain a balanced view. There are still some spectacular opportunities ahead for the relatively short range as well as for the more distant future.

The failures in progress are indeed not those of computer technology, which has an enviable enough record. Within the past ten to fifteen years the speed of the computer has been increased a thousand fold,[1] and memory capacity has multiplied by a similar ratio. At the same time, the cost of data processing has been reduced by a factor of a hundred to one. The failures are to be found rather in the human management of the machines themselves. At the same time we have been learning of the difficulties of harnessing the computer to serve our special needs, higher-level computer languages have been developing to make easier the chore of computer programming. We have learned that much of the problem of fulfillment is in understanding ourselves and our business rather than in short-comings of the machine.

COMPUTER POTENTIAL IN ADVERTISING

The range of computer capabilities in industrial production and applied science is enormous. The range within marketing and advertising may be as great, though many times more difficult of achievement. Only the narrowest possible view perceives the computer simply as a machine for bookkeeping —a function it does indeed perform with great efficiency and reliability. Few, if any, large-scale accounting operations anywhere today are unassisted by some form of electronic data processing. The prospect of a vast computer system automating the currency is not now too fantastic. Electronic banking is probably not far away. Most of the top twenty advertising agencies have on-premises computers to handle payrolls, billing and personnel data, and, as by-products, management control information. Most of the others employ service bureaus to perform this function. You may say that this type of computer employment is at the low end of the intellectual scale in that relatively low-level skills and routines are displaced. And it is, not surprisingly, at this end of the scale that the computer has been most successful in our business. The fact that the simplest tasks are disposed of first does not mean that we shall not move on to the more difficult in good time.

This broad scale of potential was perceived by advertising men early in computer history. The applications at the lower end were made very rapidly, but at the upper end of this scale they were at least identified. The analogy between computer circuitry and the human brain as drawn by the authors of cybernetics was not lost on advertising research men. The use of the computer to implement complex decision systems and to simulate marketing and advertising processes was explored. The efforts to implement such notions have not been notably successful. But the potential is undiminished. In attempting to assess our progress and understand the obstacles, we find that advertising and marketing are not unique.

Hershner Cross, a serious student of corporate management, recently did this same kind of soul-searching when he stated: "From the point of view of the general management of business . . . we are still probably only on the threshold of really significant use [of computers]," and then asked, "Now what is the reason for this slow progress?"[2] Part of his answer reads like this:

> Each of us [managers] is very obviously a product of his background, training and, of course, experience. Computers have been in broad use for only a few years and the present generation of general managers was formed much earlier.
>
> The management process, as we perform it today, is certainly heavily entrenched in the pre-computer era, and I think will require very heavy readjustments in modes of thinking, organization and methods.

While the advertising business has its special kind of professional decisions, it is equally beset with the usual problems of business management. In this area, the computer offers the opportunity, by facilitating cost control, to implement the prediction David Ogilvy made a few years ago that within five years the commission system would be displaced by a fee system in most agencies. (I bring this up only to establish the fact that creative types are no more reliable as prophets in our business than are research types—they are only more persuasive in the phrasing of their prophecies and hence longer remembered!)

Actually the inertia that Cross attributes to the mismatch of the present generation of business managers with the computer is compounded in the advertising business by the presence there of creative types. The computer demands system and logic, and these are not the essential ingredients of an advertising agency. Most self-respecting businesses refuse to house the agency function within their walls, preferring to farm it out for someone else to manage. There may even be an inverse correlation between management efficiency and advertising creativity. (This is not to say that agency profitability and creativity do not correlate.) If this view be true—that creative output and computerized decisions are incompatible —then the prospect of progress is indeed bleak. Recently I read in the Sunday *New York Times* that the creative man was rising in the agency hierarchy and was about to depose the account-executive type as the typical chief executive.

ADVERTISING DECISION-MAKING AND COMPUTERS

While I believe that Hershner Cross has correctly identified a key factor in the slowness of computer evolution in the management-decision process and that the artistic orientation of the agency business helps not at all, I would like to dig a little deeper, particularly on the occasion of this symposium of serious advertising thought. It was not alone the competitive spirit of Madison Avenue and the incessant striving for competitive advantage that surfaced and publicized the media models and their computer systems in the recent past. The promotion has faded, but the basic notions have not. There are mixed emotions and strong feelings on both sides of the issue. I have not surveyed the field exhaustively or even intensively, but I find that men, technical and research types apart, who had the opportunity to be exposed to and gain a reasonable understanding of the model-building effort place a high value on the work that has been done. Exaggerated hopes were raised, it is true, hopes that have not and perhaps never will be realized. But the net of the effort has been, in my opinion, a big plus. It has advanced considerably our understanding of the advertising process.

There are even mixed views on the current adequacy of advertising theory. Those least satisfied with our understanding of advertising on an abstract plane are those who would extend the use of the computer in decision-making. Those who are satisfied or successful with intuitive decisions have little interest in theory. The point is that without good theory, a good model cannot be built. In this sense, the terms "theory" and "model" are synonymous.

However crude may be the initial model, it offers a concrete foundation, which can be built on and constantly improved. It is a completely explicit exposition of the theoretical structure. Programmed to a computer, it becomes a working model or a working theory. Parameters of varying magnitudes can be tested. The sensitivity of variables can be determined. The theoretical constructs can be altered. All manner of "what if?" questions can be posed and answered. The computer becomes a medium for evolving and refining theory.

A good model recognizes, though it does not provide, values for its parameters and variables. And here is where progress in the employment of computers for prophesying the outcome of alternative advertising courses grinds to a halt. Some good marketing models have been built, and considerable progress in shaping a working theory of advertising has been made. Such models in the abstract perform a useful service in disciplining our thinking and in teaching us about the system, which in itself must improve the quality of decisions.

It is in the process of assigning values to the parameters that adapt the model to the special situation being evaluated—that is, bring it into line with the real-world situation—where we have been hung up. Unfortunately, the parameters of the human world, unlike the world of physics, are not invariant. For each advertising campaign, the parameters do vary significantly. In this fact lies the main obstacle to the successful employment of advertising and marketing models for decision-making. It is well enough to invest in expensive equipment to measure precisely the speed of light: its cost can be amortized over eternity. Advertising parameters are infinitely more perishable.

Still, it is useful to have parameters that are something less than as precise as the invariants of physics. Some can be approximated in experiments of affordable cost and others can be estimated by people of experience. It is, however, so often the creative types on whom we must rely for these quantified judgments, and they don't seem particularly anxious to gain experience quantifying.

Not only does the transitory nature of the advertising environment discourage the investment of time, thought, and money in computerizing the mathematical models, but it also inhibits the orderly development of advertising theory. This being the case, it seems unlikely that real progress in the understanding of the advertising process will be made unless financed from outside the operating P & L statements of agencies and advertisers or media. Even the Advertising Research Foundation will make no progress in this, its most important role, if subscribers badger that organization with demands for instant results. Proprietary interests stand in the way even of consolidating the learning that has accrued in the recent past. While the temptation is great, I shall not propose another foundation or institute to take up this important task or even a symposium or seminar or seminary.

SUB-SYSTEM MODELS

So far I have commented on the two extremes of the scale of computer capabilities in advertising decisions. One is well along the way toward achievement; the other is, at least currently, unattainable. In the middle ground lies the opportunity of the immediate future. Though the integrated marketing model may not be manageable, some of the sub-systems are. Many examples are to be found in operation today. I will mention only a few. The COMPASS model and its operating version, COUSIN, seem to be demonstrating that a limited model can produce useful results and that several agencies can jointly develop and operate a computer decision system. Russ Haley and Ron Gatty have described, in a recent publication,[3] a computer system for estimating some of the parameters of advertising variables. Many agencies are buying tapes of audience data and with their own computers or available service centers producing estimates and analyses in support of media decisions. Audience measurement services are using computer systems not only for tallying and tabulating, but also for more complex analyses of data which, in effect, are published "ready-to-wear" computer runs. One agency has as a fully developed tool a computerized sales prediction model, which substantially foreshortens the time required to establish success or failure of new products in test markets. In these examples and many others is the current payoff as well as the clue to things to come.

Measuring Consumer Goods Movements

Typical of the more modest view now held by responsible authorities was the statement made at the recent annual meeting of the 4A's by the president of a large computer software house.[4] John A. DeVries is a pussycat by comparison with the tiger who discussed the same subject at the Advertising Research Foundation annual meeting ten years ago.[5] At the earlier meeting, Professor Jay Forrester of MIT, you may recall, while disparaging the quality of advertising research, was outlining dynamic models for advertising decisions that seem as far removed from the real world today as, in fact, they did then. Forrester was indeed at the far-out end of the computer applications scale. Considering his scathing criticism of advertising decision-making in 1958, I have dreaded the thought of how he would view our progress or, in his terms, lack of it, since that time.

Mr. DeVries, on the other hand, was in good voice in the middle register. He viewed with great satisfaction the work, which is actually well advanced, in speeding up the information flow portraying consumer goods movement. The established system for brand-share score-keeping, by the nature of the store-auditing process or the consumer-diary technique that produces it, does not provide instantaneous competitive measurements. The time lag is often frustrating. Since warehouse withdrawals are, in many cases, recorded on computer tapes and since the content of such tapes can be transmitted by wire into a central computer, high-speed reporting of total warehouse shipments is readily attainable. Because such shipments anticipate movement across the checkout counter, the system goes instantaneous reporting one better—it can report consumer purchase *before* it occurs. Whether or not this is sufficient to offset some obvious deficiencies and hazards in the system remains to be established. At least, it is a real demonstration of how a computer network can generate at high speed a lot of data as a by-product of data captured for another purpose. The quality of the input is not a responsibility of the computer, although contrary to popular belief, the computer can by skillful data adjustment improve the quality of the output.

TV Spot Availabilities Exchange

In his down-to-earth view of computer usage, DeVries sees the potential of an automated exchange system for the buying and selling of television spots. This is a prospect seen by many who have speculated about the future configuration of advertising. The notion of the TV Spot Exchange combines some of both the labor-saving and the decision-making attributes of the computer. Since it is an example of the sort of computer application we may reasonably expect to affect this industry in the near future, I should like to consider it in some detail. TV spot buying and selling decisions transfer values approaching a billion dollars annually with such volumes of data, manpower, and paperwork as to weigh heavily on the profitability of the agencies and the station representatives involved.

An exchange system with large central computers and terminals in offices of buyers and sellers is technically feasible. A flow diagram of such a system would show the buyer putting into a terminal unit the specifications for buys in any number of markets, giving demographic and cost constraints along with limits on duration and positions of desired spots. When the buyer had verified his input, he would dispatch his request, not individually to the representative of each station in all his markets, but simply to the central computer. Spot availabilities best fitting the agency requirements would be selected from station inventories stored in the computer center. These lists would automatically be dispatched to the appropriate station representatives along with data indicating how well the availabilities matched the conditions specified by the buyer. The rep would edit the list, perhaps inserting price concessions, noting future program changes, and even issuing a luncheon invitation to the unseen agency buyer. The rep would then dispatch the offer to the center, presumably within the specified deadline. Back at the computer all submitted availabilities would be combined, ranked in specified order, and returned to the agency along with any additional analysis required for the individual markets, such as reach and frequency of a consolidated spot package. The orders would then be placed by the agency, confirmed by the reps, and forwarded to the stations. Finally, the spots would be run and the computer instructed to prepare the billing. Meanwhile, the agency and the rep would have on file in the data bank the source material for no end of controls and analyses.

Elements of this system are now in use on both the agency and the rep side of the exchange. The communality of hardware and software, plus savings in time, manpower, and paperwork, not to mention the increase in buying efficiency in this central system, may very well establish its economic feasibility. It should be noted that this system, in which the central element is a computer, provides a communications network in addition to performing an exchange function. The storage and retrieval of information from several different data banks comprise one of the integrated services. It is the rationalization or integration of these many parts that gives the total system special appeal and further enhances its economic value. The value of the whole is considerably greater than the sum of the parts. It should be further noted that the basic role of principal participants in the existing system is preserved by the suggested design of the new system. In my opinion, we can make the same error here that we have made before if we attempt to drive automation too far and thus eliminate important subjective judgments from the scheme of things. The man in the system, in this case, the station rep, is an essential component.

PROGRESS IN COMPUTER TECHNOLOGY

Computer applications such as a spot exchange require great capacity and high speeds to cope with peak load requirements. Computers come in all sizes and there is one best suited for each need. I just happen to be acquainted with one known in the trade as the CDC 6600, said by some to be the largest stock model in existence in the world today. *Fortune* magazine has reported that the 6600 can "multiply every number in both the 1524-page Brooklyn and 1830-page Manhattan telephone directories by the number that follows it, add the product of each of these multiplications, divide the total by any number and print out the answer in less than two seconds."[6] That may not be a terribly useful sum, but you'll have to admit that it represents a lot of arithmetic. Even if its only job were to multiply all the numbers in all the telephone directories in the world, it would have a remarkably short work week.

The progress of ten years, then, in computer application to advertising decisions has been substantial, if falling short of our original outlook. We have gained maturity in our perception of the real opportunities. Meanwhile, computer technology continues to outrun our ability to harness it. Perhaps progress will be made at a greater rate if, when the next generation of managers takes over, it is better equipped to match the next generation of computers.

NOTES

[1] Hershner Cross, "A General Management View of Computers," *Computers and Management: The 1967 Leatherbee Lectures,* Harvard Business School, Boston, 1967.

[2] *Ibid.*

[3] Russell I. Haley and Ronald Gatty, "Adapting Attitude Measurement to Computer Processing," *Computer Operations* (April–May, 1968).

[4] John A. DeVries, "Computer Technology in Marketing: A Business Management Perspective," Annual Meeting, 1968, American Association of Advertising Agencies.

[5] Jay W. Forrester, "The Relationship of Advertising to Corporate Management," Proceedings: Fourth Annual Conference, Advertising Research Foundation, October 2, 1958.

[6] *Fortune,* April, 1966, p. 165.

CHAPTER 10

Where Does Advertising Research Go from Here?

by Leo Bogart

Dr. Bogart is executive vice president and general manager of the Bureau of Advertising, American Newspaper Publishers Association. He formerly was in research positions with Standard Oil Company (New Jersey), Revlon, Inc., and McCann-Erickson. He has served as a consultant to several government agencies and conducted a year's survey of the operations of the U.S. Information Agency. He has been president of the American Association for Public Opinion Research, Radio and Television Research Council, World Association for Public Opinion Research, and Market Research Council. He has taught at Illinois Institute of Technology, New York University, and Columbia University. His books include Strategy in Advertising *and* The Age of Television.

Lately it has become very fashionable to speculate about the future, perhaps because of a growing subconscious awareness that there may not be any. As one ponders the future, it is difficult to separate one's wishful thinking from one's colder and more realistic estimates. It is in the nature of all salesmen to be optimistic, and advertising men, as a specialized strain of this breed, share the same benign affliction. So in thinking about this subject, I find it hard to disentangle my thoughts on how I would like things to happen from those on how I think they will happen.

As the last speaker of this symposium, I have prepared my remarks on the assumption that most of the important things that could be said on the subject of advertising research will already have been said by the distinguished colleagues who precede me on this platform. (That assumption has been borne out.) I have assumed also, that although my fellow-speakers were not specifically assigned to talk about the future, they would inevitably have to stress whatever they might individually regard to be the unfinished business of our profession, since to review what we know on any aspect of the subject implies that we must also review the things we don't know.

As I look at the field of advertising research, new as it is, I am impressed by how much we do know and at the same time by how much we don't know, by the richness of scholarship on which we are able to draw in the mother fields of social science, and by our continuing ignorance in some of the fundamental areas of communication and persuasion.

In looking ahead, we may take two premises for granted: (1) the world that advertising seeks to influence is changing at an ever faster rate in all its significant aspects; (2) there is also growth and change in the body of social science theory and methodology, which advertising research adapts to its own special purposes.

It sounds almost banal to refer to the major elements of change in process in the technologically advanced world of our Western society. Yet one can hardly talk intelligently about any aspect of the future without at least mentioning some of these obvious developments: an expanding population distributed spatially quite differently than it is today; a substantially higher material standard of living; better-educated people with more leisure at their disposal; an exponential growth in technology. We can ignore the more unpleasant portents, which reflect the world struggle of ideologies, and the spreading imbalance between those nations that have mastered the new technology and those that have not.

Advertising will no doubt have to adapt its character to the imminent changes in marketing institutions. These will be brought about by more rapid transportation, by decentralized and automated manufacture and distribution of standardized commodities, and eventually by the combination of televised display of merchandise in the home and feedback mechanisms that will make possible in-home shopping and computerized personal accounting.

As marketing communication expands in volume, consumer behavior will become more purposeful, and exposure to advertising more deliberately self-selective. This suggests that advertising may have to become much more informative in character and abandon some of its emphasis on mere reminder or on attempts at persuading people who have no interest in the product. At the same time, the evolution of technology will hasten the output of product innovations, and thereby enhance the importance of informative advertising as an ingredient in the marketing mix.

But advertising will also be strongly influenced by the changing technology of the media. Color will play a growing part; automation will make print media more flexible (with shorter closing dates), and more narrowly localized, as decentralized high-speed printing facilitates regional and neighborhood editions.

Most important, as I have outlined in detail in another paper,[1] I believe we will see a blurring of the line between electronics and print, as "print" can be displayed on the home videotube, with selective electrostatic recording of any excerpts desired for the permanent record. At the same time, with pre-recorded TV input condensed and transmitted in a flash to the home communications console, scanning and program choice can be speeded up for television entertainment, much as it is in print. These developments also suggest that the communication of advertising messages will become a far more selective process than it is in the media world we know today, and that the central subject matter of advertising research will shift from persuasion to information-seeking.

RESEARCHING FUNDAMENTALS

The first thing to be said about advertising research is that there isn't enough of it. One hundred and twenty-five million dollars a year (if that is a reasonable estimate) is a figure that is so modest as to be ridiculous in relation to the size of the job yet to be done, and the number of questions that remain unanswered. It is also totally inadequate when considered in relation to the potential opportunity for increasing the efficient use of the vast sums actually invested in advertising.

By any yardstick, there is tremendous variability in the performance of advertising that uses identical space or time budgets in a given medium. Suppose that through research the effectiveness of a given advertisement can be increased by 100 per cent; that the sales it generates can be doubled. How much would the research be worth?

Marginal utility theory tells us that a firm should be willing to spend additional money on advertising up to the point where the extra sales it produces yield an additional dollar of profit above and beyond the cost of manufacturing, distributing, and advertising the product, plus the cost of researching the advertising. It is worth *half* a million dollars of research funds to double the return from a one-million dollar advertising expenditure? Maybe the value added in sales efficiency is worth only a *quarter* of a million dollars. In any case, it would appear to be worth more than $7,500, but that is exactly what the average advertiser would spend on advertising research—three-quarters of one per cent of advertising expenditure.

In industry, the R & D function represents a far greater percentage of manufacturing output. In the aerospace industry, R & D budgets are 26½ per cent of sales; in the hardware end of the communications business—equipment and electrical machinery—R & D is 9½ per cent. Even in the automotive and transportation equipment field it is 3½ per cent. Yet in making material goods, the unknowns are perhaps even less formidable than they are in the field of communication and persuasion. The businessman's riposte to this argument is that his investment in advertising research might be greater if he were convinced that it would actually pay off in increased efficiency.[2] But obviously the value of the research investment in turn requires further research. Zero Mostel phrased a somewhat similar problem at the time of the Army-McCarthy hearings in a song that went, "Who will investigate the man who investigates me?"

In any case, marketing and advertising are characterized by a constant search for cheap research answers to expensive business questions, most of which cannot be answered within the framework of any individual firm's advertising research budget. Perhaps this reflects a subtle pressure on the researcher within a large corporation to emulate his corporate associates and peers by producing assembly-line statistics on a schedule of his own.

Marketers are so obsessed with the compulsion to inventory the latest figures on circulation and audience that they are prone to forget the far more important and fundamental question of what happens to their messages in the minds of the media consumers. Since the structure of advertising research puts the great burden of financing on the media, it is not surprising to find that a disproportionately large amount of the research on advertising represents the dull and repetitive measurement of media audiences, while a disproportionately small amount is concerned with actual content. Yet the leverage on successful advertising performance is vastly greater for creative research than for media research. What goes *into* an advertising message is always more idiosyncratic in content and form than the choice of the medium in which the message is to appear. The capabilities of the medium remain constant over a broad array of messages and campaigns. The content and form of a message are highly specific to the product, brand, and creative approach, and are therefore less likely to be researched.

People who practice advertising research go to the same meetings, read the same books, and exchange jobs. Perhaps for this reason, they tend to look at advertising problems as though they could be described by a uniform set of laws, and as though there were a single set of criteria for measuring what an advertisement accomplishes.

Most managements think of the dollars that they invest in advertising as expenditures that are exchanged for tangible commodities, just as in other areas of a company's operations.

This means that most businessmen concerned with advertising think of what they are buying in terms of measurable units—impressions, audience, what have you—all expressible in dollar terms by yardsticks applicable to all media. In my opinion, this way of thinking is not only unscientific, because it conflicts with our best understanding of the communications process, but also unbusinesslike, because it often leads to advertising decisions that are wrong.

The balance sheet mentality applied to the study of advertising leads to an obsessive concern with the measurement of effects, of "return on investment." Because these effects are difficult, expensive, and time-consuming to disentangle from other forces in the marketing mix, a substitute is commonly found in the study of media audiences, their size and characteristics. Studies of audience size and characteristics yield statistics that in their concreteness give the illusion of being more "actionable" than those that result from studies of *generic* problems in the communications process: varying the length or size of the message unit, the effects of repetition, patterns of repetition, flighting, etc. These *generic* problems are beyond the scope of any individual advertising research project. They require combined and collective solutions. Yet it is precisely in the handling of these elements, and the unique creative treatment of the space or time he buys, that the advertiser has the greatest leverage on the performance of his advertising.

Most advertising research is designed from the perspective of the communicator. He feels that what he has to say is extremely important. Many hours of effort go into preparing his message, and he looks at it in the screening room or board room with a different eye than that of the casual viewer or reader who takes it as it comes, in context. Most advertisers start with the assumption that their effort is always a positive force. We blind ourselves to any evidence that suggests that a great deal of selling and marketing pressure may actually be negative in its effects, and work against the interests of the seller, just as a great deal of interpersonal communication is negative in character. In human relations, it isn't always true that getting to know somebody is to love him. Very often the contrary is true. It seems to me to be particularly the case in a highly competitive market, where strong sales pressures create strong counter-pressures.

In advertising, mere reminder of the product's existence does not necessarily lead to favorable acceptance of it; familiarity is not automatically translated into a willingness to try it or buy it. With products, as with people, what we like is not necessarily what we know. The content and form of the message shape the response to it, quite apart from the ability of the medium to put it in front of the people who might be interested. The evaluation of individual ads and commercials, whether it takes the form of a portfolio test or a theater group interview, has traditionally focused on the message as the communicator sees it, in isolation and with heightened attention. One of the underdeveloped areas in advertising research is the understanding of how communications are received in their real-life setting.

In February, 1968, at the time of the Viet Cong's Tet offensive, I tuned to a television news broadcast in which film clips freshly flown over from Saigon vividly showed the agony and devastation of war in images that must have shocked and distressed any normal viewer seated comfortably in his living room. The final part of the sequence showed Colonel Loan of the South Vietnamese National Police killing a civilian-clad Viet Cong prisoner in cold blood. As the victim sank to the ground, the television screen suddenly switched to the commercial. The beaming face of an actor dressed as a filling station attendant cheerfully greeted the audience, "Hi there, I'm your friendly Phillips 66 dealer!"

It is obvious that this unfortunate juxtaposition was completely unanticipated by the advertiser and entirely unwelcome to him. However, it may serve to illustrate (1) that advertising messages and the way we react to them must always be considered in context, and (2) that most advertising is communicated in juxtaposition to our experience of the larger and more significant events of our time. Advertising research data accurately reflect the fact that many messages register negative impressions, or no impression at all on many of the people who are exposed to the sight or sound of them. Therefore, these data often seem to be at variance with the findings of the small-scale laboratory studies, most of them employing students as subjects, which are the primary source of current theoretical knowledge in experimental social psychology.

To illustrate, a cornerstone of communications research has long been the notion of selective perception, the idea that people tend to pay attention to messages that support their predispositions and to block out incongruent messages. Recently this theory has been questioned, but the experimental evidence that contradicts it is largely in the domain of highly charged subject matter, on which there are indeed opposing viewpoints. The problem must be posed quite differently in the case of messages that arouse no contradictory prior judgments, simply because they arouse no reactions at all. Perhaps the main contribution that advertising research can make to the study of communications is in the domain of inattention to low-key stimuli, as exemplified by the ever-increasing flow of unsolicited and unwanted messages to which people are subjected in our over-communicative civilization.

The twilight areas of advertising research are precisely those of social psychology in general: (1) The relation between emotional arousal or affect (both message-centered and distractive) to the transmittal of information; (2) The relation between learning information on a subject and acquiring favorable opinions of it; (3) The conditions under which favorable opinions are translated into overt behavior.

Progress in advertising research can never be in advance of our general knowledge of such subjects as the learning process, perception, motivation. But advertising research can add little to that general knowledge unless it is close to the main body of psychological experimentation and theory. Advertising research may indeed contribute useful data, and individual advertising researchers may add to the body of relevant theory. The theoretical contributions of advertising researchers however, are made largely by virtue of their academic training and orientation as social scientists, rather than in their capacities as advertising or marketing men.

THE QUALITY OF THE DATA

The assault on the unanswered questions, however, represents only a very small part of the total effort expended in advertising research. On the contrary, there seems to be a sharply heightened demand for large-scale surveys to supply the kind of repetitive data the computer can manipulate.

There will inevitably be further growth in the application of mathematical models to the solution of marketing and advertising problems. As we are all aware, the deficiencies of existing models are to be found not in the limitations of data on markets and audiences, but in the lack of clarity with regard to the basic processes of advertising communication. No doubt, the demands of the model builders will stimulate experimental research by bluntly posing questions that have always been asked, but hitherto easily evaded.

But valid models of communication will be constructed by psychologists and not by mathematicians or engineers. The present lull in activity on the great "media decisions computer model-building" front reflects the fact that the people who have had to come to grips with the problems of making the models work recognize where the areas of ignorance are, and also know that they will not be conquered easily.

The new technology of data-processing has already vastly enriched our capabilities for handling data intelligently, but it also harbors an element of danger that affects all of marketing research, not just the part of it concerned with advertising. The danger lies in the possibility of becoming so fascinated with the gadgetry that we lose sight of the flesh-and-blood realities at the bottom of all the research we do. Anyone who has ever written a master's thesis or done fieldwork for a research course knows that when you actually go out and ring doorbells and talk to people, you get subtle hues of meaning that aren't expressed in words and even less in the check-off of pre-coded answers on a questionnaire. The analytical insights that come out of those few interviews you have done yourself can never be recreated in analyzing interviews that somebody else has collected. In the very elaborate machinery of today's research, the data have become disembodied. Everybody down the line makes assumptions that the individual ahead of him did his job properly, that the interview was really conducted, that the answers were correctly recorded, that they were properly coded, that the girl who verified the punching didn't goof, that there were no mistakes in computation, that the analyst's judgment was sound in what he chose to present in his report to the user.

The computer makes it possible to cross-tabulate every item in a survey by every other item, studying the relationships between "everything and everything." This raises a real threat that the researcher may become smothered in more data than he can possibly analyze intelligently and efficiently.

Even more serious is the possibility that the data may be taken as ends in themselves. Some of us worry far too little about the quality of what went into the computer in the first place and worry a great deal more than we should about analytical constructs in the output, which represent mathematical abstractions rather than human truths.

Along with this comes a tendency to demand more and more data to feed the insatiable demands of the machine. We need larger studies, with more interviews to handle the increased number of variables that the computer allows us to manipulate or hold constant. At the same time, the fieldwork controls over increased number of interviews often tend to receive proportionately less top-level attention.

In the past few years, there has been a proliferation of the syndicated services that offer consumption and media data. The resulting profile-matching of media and markets is sometimes based on small subsamples, which no longer represent the universe that they purport to measure with the kind of precision that would seem to be required by the huge investment decisions they influence.

The tremendous apparatus of today's marketing research has created powerful vested interests in the big numbers for which advertisers pay so much. Consider the case of the TV ratings, whose value in measuring program share of audience no one can question. Over a year ago it was pointed out that there are discrepancies of the order of 70 per cent between the audience size projected from the most widely used national syndicated service and the audience size found in a very large one-time personal coincidental interview survey. The one key point of rebuttal to this observation was the allegation that some people watching TV may not have wished to open their doors to an interviewer. This argument was demolished in a follow-up study for *Life* magazine, which used an electronic detection device to check the validity of the interview findings. In addition, further evidence has accumulated regarding the disparity between TV audience size projections based on meters, diaries, and telephone coincidental interviews.

Let us hope that on the immediate future agenda of advertising research there will be room for a study of broadcast ratings methodology that matches the quality and scope of the All-Radio Methodology Study. But what seems to me to be much more central to the subject matter of advertising research is *not* the question of whether the ratings are overstated by 70 per cent, or 28 per cent, or 10 per cent, but the question of why and how the powers that be have thus far successfully resisted any searching attempt to learn the truth.

When this subject was raised last year, it was immediately brushed off as a self-serving competitive attack on the part of one medium versus another. No particular interest in exploring this discrepancy was shown by the corporations who spend millions of dollars a year to buy TV rating services, and nearly three billion dollars a year on TV advertising schedules planned on the basis of ratings and premised on their accuracy. The Association of National Advertisers rejected an offer of funds to help initiate a comparison of TV research methods. *Life's* follow-up study was presented to the Advertising Research Foundation conference in the fall of 1967; it has since been circulated by the ARF to its membership, and it won the top Media/Scope research award. Yet it has been virtually ignored by the advertising and broadcasting trade press. Nor was there any indignant reaction in advertising circles when the board chairman and president of a great broadcasting network persisted in disseminating to advertising opinion leaders a public statement contrary to the known facts about the TV-viewing habits of different income sectors of the public—long after their original error had been pointed out. These incidents simply illustrate the enormous resistance on the part of many researchers to any critical questioning of the numbers that are their stock in trade, which they spend so many hours poring over month after month and quarter after quarter. Maturity in the profession of advertising research will come when researchers change the attitude that they are merely paid to deal with the numbers as they are ground out and can't be concerned with looking behind them.

THE STUDY OF THE ADVERTISING SYSTEM

When I say that advertising research should be concerned with the very phenomenon of its own practitioners' rejection of unpleasant questions, I am really voicing what I believe to be the main point of this paper, which is that the proper study of advertising research is the advertising system, and not advertisements. Advertising research has been mainly concerned with the evaluation of techniques of persuasion borrowed from other fields of mass communication. It has been concerned only incidentally with the peculiar institutions of advertising itself.

In my opinion, these institutions, no less than the processes of advertising communication, represent a most rewarding and largely neglected target for study. In fact, they may well be the unique subject matter of advertising research. These institutions demand attention, not merely because of the vast expenditure that goes to maintain them in the United States and throughout the Western world, but also because of their extraordinary significance in the functioning of the entire marketing system and of the mass media, which shape public information, public opinion, and national character.

Except for books and motion pictures, all the mass media are dependent primarily on advertising for their income; advertisers' support of the media is in turn contingent upon their proven ability to fill the entertainment and information needs of the public. Considered in this light, advertising would appear to be merely an element in a continuous cycle through which public demand is satisfied by media that cater to popular interests, in which the availability of audiences with distinctive and definable characteristics presents advertisers with economically efficient opportunities for marketing communication, and in which advertisers' requirements inevitably push the media to maximize their responsiveness to the demands of their particular publics.

However, matters are not quite that simple, since some media enjoy what are in effect unique positions that give advertisers no option except to use them. Moreover, all media exercise some editorial options to present unpopular subject matter or to appeal to minority or special-interest groups.

Years ago Upton Sinclair, in a scathing indictment of the American press, *The Brass Check*, suggested that many newspapers of his day venally corrupted the presentation of the news to serve advertisers' interests.[3] Some years later George Seldes advanced a more qualified argument to the effect that there was no reason for overt slanting, since the values and views of the advertising businessman were apt to be identical with those of the publisher businessman.[4] This notion would be greeted with hollow laughter today by the advertising staff of any good newspaper, who are in some cases barely permitted civil contact with the editorial side.[5]

But the relation between advertisers and the content of the media has taken on new subtleties since the development of broadcasting. The size of the broadcast audience is almost inelastic. At 7 o'clock this evening, a certain number of people in this country will flick on their television sets. Plus or minus a few per cent, the same number will turn them on whether they can watch only one channel, two channels, or if they can watch seven channels—unless there are extraordinary changes in the programming content. For example, if the President is going to deliver a major address and all three networks broadcast it, the occasional independent station which reruns an old movie will have its audience share zoom, though the total level of viewing may drop somewhat. The absolute level of audience size is governed mainly by the daily time cycle of activities. Bad programming will almost always drive out the good, because the bad is almost always easier to take than the good. If there's a choice between a rerun of the Lucy show and a Senate committee hearing, most people will switch to the Lucy show. If the choice were always limited to programming, total audience size would not suffer.

So we are faced with "the great debate over cultural democracy,"[6] on the issue of whether to give people what is good for them or what they want. The advertiser inevitably wants people to get what they want from the media, since it would seem to assure that they will stay as part of the audience, and since he is inclined to believe that the physical presence of a warm human body within reach of his message represents an opportunity for persuasion.

The overriding concern with numbers creates pressure for media content to be governed by the formulas that have proved successful in building them. It discourages experimentation, and arouses inordinate concern about antagonizing any minority segment of the audience.

Advertisers have become less and less identified with TV programming content as "scatter plans" for widely disseminating commercial messages have replaced the older tradition of program sponsorship. Sponsorship was based on the premise that an advertiser's confirming identification with a program created favorable associations quite apart from the immediate sales effect of any individual commercial. Only a handful of companies, primarily utilities and industrial advertisers, have maintained an enlightened policy of sponsoring public service programs over long periods of time.

Most news and public affairs operations must be carried by the television networks at a considerable loss. The American Broadcasting Company lost $2,000,000 on a much-heralded four-hour documentary on Africa. This episode must surely have had some influence on the network's decision not to broadcast the political conventions of 1968 live in their entirety.

The content of our mass media is determined today by a businesslike appraisal of how to avoid rocking the boat, a boat in which advertiser interest and public acceptance often sit at opposite ends. The personal tastes of the decision-maker must be totally subordinated to his business judgment, and may even be in sharp contrast to it.

This state of affairs is remote indeed from the origins of mass media as vehicles of individual expression. When Addison and Steele wrote their journals of London life, they set down what they wanted to say, whatever struck them as being of note or of interest, and not necessarily what would appeal to the greatest possible number of readers. Even in our own day, some media like the "little magazines" and underground movies operate on this principle, which brings them into the tradition of high culture in which individual expression is paramount.

As the technology of communication has become more complex, starting with the rotary press and the linotype and moving into the era of the vacuum tube and the transistor, proportionately greater resources have had to be applied to the mechanics of producing and distributing the product, relative to the creation of its content. Someone has had to pay for the machinery and the wages of those who operate it. Thus begins the spiral of interdependence between advertiser economic support, audience size, and the satisfaction of majority tastes. It is hard to visualize anything other than an acceleration of this process in the future as communications technology becomes infinitely more sophisticated and as even greater financial resources are required to sustain it.

Thus the mass media have a penetrating influence on the political process as well as on the quality and direction of the national culture, and on the public's conception of what is good and true and beautiful. And these mass media depend on advertiser support and operate within limits which advertisers set.

Studies of the press and foreign policy have shown that the *New York Times* occupies a highly unique position of authority. It is widely read by most high officials of the federal administration and by members of Congress and the foreign diplomatic corps. Its indirect influence, equally important, reflects a reliance on the *Times*' editorial treatment on the part of executives in other news media.

I cannot assess, and perhaps no one can, the effect on the

Times' internal editorial councils of the changes of the past few years on the New York newspaper scene. The daily problem of writing and editing the *Times* copy has undoubtedly been strongly affected by the demise of the *Herald-Tribune*. Nowhere is this problem more keenly felt than in criticism of the arts—theater, motion pictures, books, ballet, paintings, and music—in which the voices of *Times* reviewers are often virtually unchallenged in the nation's principal cultural center.

The death of other New York newspapers came about from very complex causes, but lack of readership was not one of them. Millions of people read the *Herald-Tribune*, the *World-Telegram and Sun*, the *Journal-American*, and the *Mirror* every day, up to their respective last days, and a large proportion of them read several papers and got several points of view on the same subjects. In deciding not to give these papers the support they needed to survive, advertisers followed judgments based on an assessment of their short-run self-interest. I am skeptical that these judgments were based on the solid evidence of careful sales analysis or market research. But the ultimate consequences—the limitations on media choice—were not in the advertisers' interests.

My argument is that self-interested, short-term–perspective decisions by individual advertisers add up to large-scale collective controls that profoundly affect the whole American cultural and political experience. These individual decisions are also crucial to the American consumer market, which, like our culture, is something more than the sum of all its separate parts. For most consumer goods and for many industrial goods, advertising is an essential catalytic agent within the complex sales and marketing structure of our economy.

About a year ago, I had a visit in East Berlin with a youngish professor who has spent his entire adult life under the present regime and is a true believer. He had recently made his first trip into the West, as part of an exchange visit of intellectuals with the Federal Republic. I asked him what had struck him most about this experience, and he replied immediately and with great distaste, "the constant goading to consume—the signs, the displays, the advertising." Advertising has been somewhat rehabilitated in East Germany as elsewhere in Eastern Europe, so his revulsion was not so much on ideological grounds as on the basis of his own strong ascetic puritanism: he really felt it was wrong for people to be constantly reminded of material things, to be importuned to buy them from all sides.

Apart from what a specific advertising campaign does for a specific product, there is a broader combined effect of the thousands of advertising exhortations that confront every consumer in America each day, the constant reminder of material goods and services not yet possessed. That effect at the level of individual motivation is felt in a constant impetus toward more consumption, toward acquisition, toward upward mobility. At the collective level it is felt in the economic drive to produce and to innovate, which fuels our economic system.

The economic, cultural, and political consequences of advertising go far beyond the dimensions of a $17 billion-a-year industry, substantial as those dimensions are in themselves. If we could reduce all advertising activities to the preparation and dissemination of sales messages for particular products, we might perhaps be justified in regarding the primary task of advertising research as one of perfecting the technology of advertising communication. We would be perfectly correct to define the mission of our profession as ancillary to the larger mission of making advertising expenditures more efficient and more rational. The efficiency of advertising as a business investment is, indeed, our subject matter, and represents the most logical source of support for our projects.

I don't think we should accept this narrow definition of the subject simply because it represents the easiest job description. Why don't we start with the big picture, with a view of advertising as a tremendous institution, which deserves study in its own right because of its influence on the most vital concerns and powers and values of our society?

If we redefine the subject in this way, a number of subjects come to the forefront, which might not otherwise have occurred to us. We must become more interested in studying the processes by which advertising decisions are made within the corporation and the advertising agency. We must seek to define the assumptions that underlie these decisions and determine to what degree they are really justified by the evidence. We must be concerned with evaluating the way in which media subject matter reflects advertisers' directives and judgments and assumptions, both directly and indirectly. We should be investigating conflicts of role on the part of media decision-makers (e.g., the TV producer who won't have a TV set in the house). We should be enlisting the support of cultural critics and historians, as well as psychiatrists, to study the influence of advertising on the fantasy life of the public, on its conscious aspirations and unconscious motives. We should be probing the symbolism evoked by the models and scenes depicted in advertising to see what impact they have had on the national character.

Anyone who has ever taken a copy of *Life* to the Soviet Union or to any underdeveloped country learns very quickly that ads carry many kinds of information and influence beyond those intended by the people who write them and lay them out.

Few studies have attempted to code and interpret the symbolism of advertisements in different media and product categories in terms of such criteria as the emphasis on people versus products, the sex, age, appearance, and probable ethnicity of the models portrayed, the setting or background, the type of copy appeal employed, the difficulty or simplicity of the language, the ratio of adjectives and adverbs to verbs and nouns in the body text, and the multitude of other variables commonly employed in the critical analysis of literature or art. Such content analysis might be a lot cheaper to conduct than a good deal of media audience research, and provide for better clues to distinguish successful from unsuccessful ads.

We can now make only impressionistic statements about the meanings advertising conveys in our society, meanings that establish its real function and place. Research into the iconography of advertising would lead us to a far better assessment of how these meanings complement, or differ from, other elements in the popular culture of which they form a very salient part.

Since Watts, it has become commonplace to observe that

when riots erupt in the inner city, the looters simply act out the acquisitive urges that they had been exhorted to follow by advertising. Advertising provides the underprivileged individual with notions of what constitutes the good life, and thus enhances his awareness of his own deprivations. People of low income may be comparatively underexposed to the colorful advertisements in the popular magazines, but they are heavy viewers of television, whose verbal exhortations to consume are hard to evade, and confront the viewer directly.

But an even more interesting and subtle connection has been traced between advertising and America's racial crisis. For some thirty years, social psychologists concerned with Negro personality and self-image have stressed the traumatic and degrading effect of the discovery in the life of each Negro child that "God is white," a discovery reinforced by his experiences with the wider world as this is represented by the mass media. But the world of the mass media, which could look fairly remote to the Southern rural or small-town Negro of times past, is a world of great immediacy in the Northern big city slum, with its blaring loudspeakers and its intense interpenetration of the immediate environment and the urban background of television programming.[7]

Social scientists have often commented on the absence or low incidence of Negroes in the mass media, except in stereotyped roles. Changes in the political climate during the post-World War II period brought about a sharp decline in ethnic stereotyping of all kinds. As a result, in the fifties Negro actors found diminishing employment in the movies and TV, until in the sixties the pendulum swung back, perhaps creating an overeagerness to cast them only as psychoanalysts and space scientists.

Of 8,280 commercials monitored in 1967 for the New York City Commission on Human Rights, only 190 included a "minority group" performer, and 49 of these were public service announcements. The hearings held by the commission coincided with the aftermath of urban violence and the consequent (and belated) awareness of racial issues on the part of large corporations. The result has been a rapid increase in the use of

Negro models and actors in ads and commercials (as well as in the employment of Negroes in what has traditionally been a nearly all-white industry).

Is it really beyond the province of advertising research to consider the effects of advertising's choice of hero figures, social backgrounds, and symbolic content on the minds, motivations, aspirations and emotions of the public? To do so would mean transcending the particular ad, or campaign, to which advertising researchers commonly address themselves. It would require an effort to deal broadly with the whole body of advertising as a force in the creation of national collective unconscious.

With $30 billion a year being spent on the Vietnam war, plus countless dozens of millions by the networks and advertisers to support the presentation of the TV newscasts that have brought the realities of the war home to the American public, maybe it would be worth, say, $150,000 to investigate the real communications impact of television on so vital a subject. Why isn't it being done? Because there's no immediate payoff to any one interested party. There's much more of a payoff for someone to study the size of audiences for the 7 o'clock newscasts of network A versus network B, and thereby to demonstrate to a prospective advertiser that Huntley-Brinkley have a better rating than Cronkite, or vice-versa.

To the extent that advertising research includes such larger matters of inquiry as these within its domain, it will inevitably become quite a different field of study, and attract quite a different breed of student—and professor. Advertising research must inevitably be limited in its intellectual aspirations so long as its concerns are microscopic, so long as the field essentially reflects an engineering, "how-to-do-it" approach to the solution of particular advertising problems. So long as the researcher acts merely as an orderly to the skillful practitioner of advertising, he must accept the values and goals of the people who pay his bills. Inevitably, any applied research that is intended to give practical help to a decision-maker must be handicapped by its inability to question the decision-maker's motives or wisdom or fundamental assumptions.

Research on a great social institution can never be conducted from the position of the Establishment. The only useful picture is an objective one. But to be objective, the researcher can hardly fail to be critical in spirit, to question all articles of faith, and therefore to risk appearing heretical to the high priests of the institutions that are the objects of his research as well as its patrons.

NOTES

[1] "Mass Media in the Year 2000," *Gazette,* Vol. 13, No. 3 (1967).

[2] I am indebted to Lester Frankel for this observation.

[3] *The Brass Check; A Study of American Journalism* (New York: Albert & Charles Boni, 1936).

[4] *Lords of the Press* (New York: Julian Messner, Inc., 1938).

[5] The May, 1968 issue of *Harper's* carries an interesting article on "The Perils of Publishing" by John Fischer, which documents the degree to which editors of reputable publications are immune to direct advertising pressures.

[6] See Bernard Berelson. "The Great Debate over Cultural Democracy," in Donald N. Barrett (Ed.), *Values in America* (South Bend, Ind.: University of Notre Dame Press, 1961).

[7] "The Marketer as a Radical," *Conference Board Record,* October, 1968, pp. 22–23.

III. FRONTIERS OF ADVERTISING EDUCATION

CHAPTER 11

Some Observations about Advertising Education

by C. H. Sandage

Dr. Sandage is professor, emeritus, and former head of the Department of Advertising, at the University of Illinois. He continues as president of the Farm Research Institute and a consultant to various firms. His books include Advertising Theory and Practice, Radio Advertising for Retailers, The Role of Advertising, The Promise of Advertising, *and* Readings in Advertising and Promotion Strategy. *He has received wide recognition for his contributions to advertising and advertising education (see biographical note at the beginning of this book).*

1968 is a memorable year in Illinois history. The state is observing its 150th anniversary and the University is celebrating its centennial. The history of advertising education is not so memorable nor does it reach back so far. Two-thirds of a century is about as much as can be claimed.

It was in 1902 that Witt K. Cochrane opened in Chicago what he called a College of Advertising. About this same time the International Correspondence Schools added advertising to its list of courses.

While these were essentially trade-school operations, they helped to draw attention to the substantial growth of advertising in the country and to the need for some degree of expertise in the shaping and styling of advertisements.

These and other aspects of advertising began to arouse the curiosity and interest of some young professors in orthodox academic institutions. These young men were located at several universities and represented different academic disciplines. The universities of primary influence were Minnesota, Northwestern, Wisconsin, Missouri, Michigan, and Washington. The professors included Harlow Gale, Walter Dill Scott, Daniel Starch, H. F. Adams, J. P. Powell, Merle Thorp, and Hugh Agnew.

GROWTH OF A NEW ACADEMIC DISCIPLINE

From these early beginnings what has become recognized as an academic discipline of advertising was born. The father of this child was psychology and the mother, journalism. It might, therefore, be said of advertising education that its sire was psychology and its dam journalism.

In many respects the offspring of this parentage had a troubled childhood. The child was abandoned by its father at an early age, but business-marketing moved in as a sort of stepfather to share with journalism the task of rearing the child in its formative years. There was some conflict in the family as to how the child should be brought up. One parent thought it should be nurtured on a diet of creativity, while the other recommended a menu closely related and subservient to the marketing aspects of business. Both parents viewed the child as chattel and directed its life toward serving the particular interests of journalism and business.

Under these circumstances education in advertising was confined primarily to offering students individual courses that were essentially descriptive and trade-oriented. In journalism such courses were related to the media and particularly to newspapers. In business they were related primarily to the area of selling and distribution. Emphasis was on how to write copy, how to develop a layout, how to reproduce an ad, how to sell space, how to select media. It was almost all *how* and little or no *why*. The approach was perhaps helpful in training "bricklayers," but of little value in developing "architects."

During the adolescent period of advertising education serious questions began to be asked. What was the nature of this thing called advertising? Was it just a tool of business and a source of revenue for the press? Did it have a vital part to play in the total economic structure of a free enterprise system? What was its impact on society as a whole? Did it provide essential benefits to consumers? Could it perform particular economic and social functions more effectively than could other agencies, and what might those functions be? What skills would be needed by those engaged in implementing the functions of advertising?

Wrestling with these and other questions helped advertising education grow to young adulthood. It perhaps reached that stage only a decade or so ago. Certainly not all questions have been answered and many have not yet even been asked. But enough intellectual ferment has been engendered to produce meaningful dialogue and debate, to stimulate a flow of literature that bears upon this area, and to provide a significant start in bringing together a body of knowledge that serves as a foundation on which the new discipline of advertising is being built.

In its adulthood advertising education is fast becoming recognized as an independent member of the academic community. It may still sleep in the family house, but it is no longer chattel of either parent. In terms of the amoeba-like evolution of academic disciplines, advertising is splitting from its parents as marketing split from economics, journalism from English, and psychology from philosophy.

CONCERNS OF THE ADVERTISING CURRICULUM

The academic discipline of advertising must be concerned with many things. It must concern itself with advertising as an institution in our social and economic order and also with the field of professional advertising practice. These two cannot be effectively separated. A particular area of societal needs is related to the institution, and the means for meeting those needs is related to the practitioner. The latter cannot perform well without knowledge and understanding of what need is to be met.

The institutional nature of advertising is not universally understood. Institutions are creations of man. They are sometimes created by law but often develop only an informal structure. The basic concept, however, is that society, formally or informally, assigns to an institution certain functions to be performed in the common good.

In our modern economic structure society recognizes the need to have broad distribution of information about goods and services available for human consumption. This need is particularly apparent in a free market system, but is present in socialistic systems as well. The substantial mobility of consumers and the great diffusion of product sources that characterize modern society enhance the need for the dissemination of product and service information. This need is multiplied when new products are continually being developed for entry into the marketplace. The right of the consumer to have information about products is as fundamental as the right of the citizen to have news about social and political happenings. The institution of advertising has assumed or been assigned the task of performing this function of disseminating product information to buyers in the marketplace.

Society also recognizes, although many people are reluctant to admit it, that there is a need for a persuasive force to encourage, stimulate, pressure, or cajole consumers to try the new and to stretch their wants. This is especially true in an affluent society and in one which has established full employment as a national goal. This function to persuade has been assumed by or assigned to advertising.

A third function of advertising is a little more cloudy and perhaps only recently recognized as a social need. That is the function of education in consumerism. There is a difference between consumption and consumerism. The former places emphasis on consumption for its own sake or for the sake of keeping people employed or for the sake of clearing the warehouses of the manufacturer or the shelves of the distributor. Consumerism involves consumption geared to the needs and wants of consumers and designed to maximize consumer satisfactions.

It appears that society wants advertising to assume the function of educating society in the art of consumerism. It may be, however, that advertising will fail in this area and some other institution will be assigned the task of implementing this function. It should be abundantly clear that the function needs to be performed by some agency of society, and advertising has a golden opportunity to serve society in this area.

Some in both government and advertising seem to think that consumerism is basically antagonistic to the concept of business free enterprise. Spokesmen from both areas have sometimes failed to recognize the basic function of both business and government.

It is, in a way, strange that this conflict in point of view should exist. Adam Smith, almost two centuries ago, said "consumption is the sole end and purpose of all production; and the *interest* of the producer ought to be attended to only so far as it may be necessary for promoting that [the *interest*] of the consumer." The very essence of consumerism is contained in that quotation.

The principle of the free enterprise system is that businessmen are self-appointed employees of consumers. As such they attend to the needs and wants of consumers. In respect to advertising this would mean that if the employer (consumer) wants more information about products, wants information of a particular kind, wants new products to meet unsatisfied needs, wants truth and honesty in the communication channels, and wants encouragement to experiment with the new, then the employee (advertiser) should devote his energies to meeting those wants. The theory of capitalism is that he who best serves the consumer will be most abundantly rewarded. Thus, the very heart of our capitalistic economic system provides the building blocks for the structure of consumerism.

Non-capitalistic economic systems are also, ideologically, organized to serve the consumer. Whether it be government under a socialistic or communistic system, or private business under a free market system, the presumed economic goal is to serve the needs and wants of consumers.

There are, of course, many consumers who are consumption illiterates, that is, they cannot effectively relate real need or want to products in the marketplace. There is much to be done to erase consumption illiteracy. It is not unlikely that advertising can and does contribute to a reduction of such illiteracy. Of course, consumption illiterates are easy prey for the short-sighted and opportunistic businessman. They need the protection of the government as a policeman. In the long run a program designed to raise the level of understanding and sophistication of consumers would be infinitely better. It would seem this is one of the opportunities and responsibilities of advertising.

The advertising practitioner who strives to implement the concept of consumerism will be empathetic to consumer needs and wants. He will recognize that through his actions he has the power to add utility to a product or service. The utility that he adds might be called information utility. Other kinds of utility that are familiar in the literature of economics include form, place, and time utility. The manufacturer can increase the satisfaction consumers receive from lumber by forming it into a chair. To maximize satisfaction the chair must conform to the physical and mental characteristics and desires of the consumer. It must not be so fragile that it will break under normal weight, nor so small that it cannot accept one's body. In short, form utility is greatest when the product is designed to meet a human need, want, or desire.

The same is true for information utility. To the person who is allergic to milk (and there are millions in the U.S.), the utility of a loaf of bread is increased when the advertising or the label carries the information that the bread contains no milk. In this age of mechanical household appliances many housewives do not receive maximum utility from the use of such appliances because information on how to use them or on various ways in which they can be used is inadequate. Information utility like form utility is greatest when keyed to human need, want, or desire.

EDUCATION *FOR* ADVERTISING

And what have these things got to do with advertising education? A great deal. First, there is education *about* advertising. The lay citizen would be in a better position to use advertising and exercise greater influence on how it is used if he has some understanding of what functions it is supposed to perform.

Then there is education *for* advertising. Here attention is given to educating young men and women who hope to become advertising practitioners. They, too, must know the functions to be performed since these serve as the foundation on which their field of practice is built. Such understanding will provide them with the *why*, and breathe life and purpose into the exercise of their skills.

But education *for* advertising must go beyond the recognition and understanding of functions. It must be professional in nature. It should include training in the various skills students will need to effectively pursue their work as communicators, persuaders, and educators in consumerism. There is no need to go into detail in respect to what skills courses should be provided in a program of professional education except to observe that they would include work in message construction, media evaluation and selection, campaign planning and strategy, advertising management, and research methods.

The current status of advertising education is such that universities have not yet accepted the responsibility for doing the full job of preparing professionals for the field. Today, universities provide the philosophical and theoretical foundations plus basic training in skills, but depend on business firms to provide interne training. This is not necessarily bad except that it has sometimes developed confusion between education and training. Some industry people tend to place major emphasis on the trade or craft aspects of preparation and little or no emphasis on theory, philosophy, functions, and problem-solving—all elements that are basic to understanding and thus to education.

Need for More Professionalism

The future may well see a greater degree of integration of the work offered by university departments of advertising and the work of an interne nature provided by those in the field of practice.

Advertising education can learn much from a study of some of the other fields of professional education. The field of medicine might be used as an example. Medicine has come a long way from the day of the witch doctor and the community midwife. But in the process of growth many practices were followed and taught that were later found to be fallacious, dangerous, or unnecessary. One need only recall the practice of bleeding patients to remove bad blood, indiscriminate removal of tonsils and appendixes, blind dependence on antibiotics, and long immobilization of surgery patients, to recognize the truth of this observation. The prospect of improper diagnosis of a patient's ills is increased when diagnosis is done by a poorly educated and trained physician.

What then can we expect from a poorly educated and trained advertising man? Will he know how to measure the temperature of consumer need and desire? Will he know how to diagnose the want-satisfying qualities of products in terms of consumer need? Even if the diagnosis is correct, will his knowledge and understanding be sufficient to prescribe a formula that will bring buyer and seller together in the most efficient manner and to the benefit of both? Will he, through ignorance, at times prescribe a blood-letting or an unnecessary operation?

Of course, this is happening in the field of advertising. The way to reduce this situation is to increase our understanding of problems and solutions. The modern and scientific approach toward greater understanding is through research. Experiment, test, and measure results under controlled conditions. Advertising education must more and more concern itself with research. This will require the combined efforts of educators and practitioners. Progress in this area could be hastened if research by practitioners were to be pooled and made available to analysts and theoreticians and made a part of the public domain. Much good could come also from the establishment of university-based research centers, perhaps operated on a cooperative basis.

Advertising education must look to the future as well as to the past and present. There should be some educators in the field of advertising who function as theoreticians, analysts of trends, and critics of current practice. History indicates that the beacon light of progress has been carried more often by researchers and academically minded people than by others in society. It is to be hoped that educators in the field of advertising will, in the future, do their share in lighting the way of progress.

It is significant that the American Association of Advertising Agencies recently established the Educational Foundation to give moral and financial support to research in advertising at the university level. It is encouraging to note that the Foundation is concentrating its full effort on supporting basic research in advertising. This is tangible evidence that professionals in the field of practice are interested in knowing more about the power and influence of advertising as a social and economic force—more about the *why* of advertising.

Social and Industry Criticism

Another facet of advertising education involves the element of social or industry criticism. The industry needs the critic—particularly the critic that is constructive. Of course, not all advertising practitioners are meeting the charge that society has given them. Also, there are undoubtedly practices now followed that are inimical to top efficiency. The detached position of the professional advertising educator places him in an effective position to serve as constructive critic. Such criticism may be inadequate today, but advertising education must include this as one of its responsibilities.

Emphasis has been given here to the institutional aspects of advertising as well as to the professionals who are involved in implementing the functions assigned to the institution. It should be borne in mind that an institution is a viable thing and its nature and purpose can change. Functions which it now performs may be taken over by some other institution or it may have its responsibilities expanded to include other functions.

It would appear that this is now happening in the case of advertising. Thus, the function of education in consumerism may be taken over by some other agency if advertising practitioners do not perform in this area as society expects.

Advertising and Dissemination of Speech

It appears that another function is now being assigned to advertising by society. This is the function of modernizing and making effective the basic desire of democratic society for freedom to speak. Modern society has become so mobile and diffused that the old instruments for effecting the dissemination of one's speech are no longer adequate. The number of people who can be reached by speaking in the town square, even with the use of a bullhorn or public address system, is extremely limited. To make freedom of speech effective, some method must be developed for making modern facilities for the dissemination of speech available.

Such facilities are at hand in the form of white space and blank time in the mass media. Thus, advertising is beginning to assume the function of dissemination of speech that deals with matters not related to products or commercial services. Not only does it serve as disseminator, but advertising practitioners also serve to translate the citizen's speech into language keyed to the idiom of the audience. In many respects advertising practitioners might be looked upon as "professional communicators for hire." This is not unlike the lawyer whose professional service is available to plead the case of a client. The future may well see a great increase in this area of advertising.

We have traveled far from the time Witt Cochrane opened the Chicago College of Advertising. During that interval advertising education has grown from a largely descriptive, skills-oriented approach to an approach that is both socially functional and professionally oriented. It is taking its place in the college community as a separate and independent academic discipline. It has not forgotten its heritage, but it no longer serves only the interests of its parents. Its future will depend largely on the intellectual quality of those who choose to devote their time and talent to it. We are dealing with a powerful force and as yet know not enough of how it works and why. The need is great for scholars, both within and without the universities, to further understanding. I am confident the challenge will be met.

CHAPTER 12

A New Look at Advertising Education

by William A. Marsteller

Mr. Marsteller is chief executive officer of Marsteller Inc., Marsteller Research, and Burson-Marsteller, Inc. Before establishing his own agency, he served in advertising and marketing executive positions with Edwards Valves, Inc., and the Rockwell Manufacturing Company. He has been a president of the National Association of Industrial Advertisers (now Association of Industrial Advertisers) and a director of the American Association of Advertising Agencies.

The thesis I wish to advance is not a popular one. Very few educators, outside the ranks of the teachers of advertising, accept it. That in itself ought to make it popular with business, but oddly it is not. In short, I believe that the trend toward simply a broad cultural education as preparation for a career in communications is a bad trend.

That's my thesis, oversimplified. Now let's see if it has any substance.

So far as I am able to determine, the history of the teaching of advertising has followed a pattern not unlike the teaching of any other relatively narrow occupational specialty, except for the professions. It found favor in the large tax-supported universities, especially the land-grant colleges that were founded on a tradition of teaching agricultural and mechanical arts, and by easy extrapolation, various other commercial specifics.

It tended to be housed in Colleges of Commerce or Schools of Journalism, usually the latter, and was often barely tolerated in either abode.

It gained curriculum permanency, along with other untraditional courses, during the depression when even a journalism school graduate was held to be more employable than a liberal arts major, who in those hard days was believed to have learned nothing practical and to be marked with the additional stigma of not knowing what he wanted out of life.

The depression was almost a trade-school climate. Benign conditions resulted in the proliferation of embarrassingly narrow, craft-oriented courses often taught by unprepared tutors who were more weedy than tweedy.

On this period I can be autobiographical. The University of Illinois was regarded then, as it is now, as one of the half-dozen best in the land for getting an education in advertising and communications. I was graduated from the School of Journalism with a B.S. (Before Sandage) as an editorial major and an advertising minor, with a fairly typical record. Among other credentials were these:

1. I had quite high grades, not too surprisingly since in three courses I was paid 40 cents an hour by the NYA to grade papers while taking the course.
2. I had credit hours in several exceptional fields, including newspaper morgue-keeping, current events, and advertising layout, which turned out to be house organ layout because the man who taught it had never done anything else.
3. I had gotten through my last two years without owning, renting, or borrowing a textbook of any kind.
4. I had a job on a local newspaper, where a man who taught me a course in advertising copy five days a week worked for me on a copy desk on Saturday.

Now as I say, the University of Illinois was one of the best. In some schools, things were a little sloppy and unprofessional.

Seriously, advertising education everywhere was a paste-pot and scissors kind of operation. It is not surprising that it was often scorned by responsible educators, and by men like me who more or less wasted college years in non-taxing exposure to corners and pieces of what is a very real, very rewarding, and very sophisticated wide world of communications.

Now we have had a wide swing. It has become popular to declare that the universities must give only the cultural base to which industry will, on the job, add the craft competence.

This assumes several things:

First, that the advertising industry is equipped to teach craft competence on a broad enough basis to support its personnel needs.

Second, that industry can (and indeed is willing to) teach anything that the university can.

And third, that the university's teaching probably won't be as good as industry can provide.

I think all three assumptions are false.

It is becoming increasingly apparent that not as many as 50 advertisers and advertising agencies combined now have or are likely to have any kind of formal training programs. Of these, I am aware of only two advertisers and less than a dozen advertising agencies where the program is complete enough or long-running enough to develop any measurable degree of advertising expertise in more than one or two sub-specialties. Since industry employment is growing at a rate far beyond the capacity of this limited training effort, advertisers and agencies are going to have to depend on others. Even the agency heads who have had intoxicating love affairs with the Harvard Business School or inexact facsimiles thereof on the one hand, or Swarthmore or whatever on the other, are sending their recruiters in increasing numbers to mingle with the advertising majors at Illinois, Missouri, Northwestern, Wisconsin, NYU, and other such places, fouling things up for those of us who have known that that is where the action is all the time.

The second assumption—that industry can and is willing to teach what the university should—is the area I would like to deal with in a little depth.

There are four broad subjects that can and ought to be present in college advertising teaching programs, that are rarely to be found in industry training programs. They are the ethics, economics, aesthetics, and social and commercial relationships of advertising. They are the kind of subject matter to be found in heavy doses in the teaching of the professions. Let us examine them individually.

First, ethics, and let's include not purely moral considerations, but the more subjective area of good taste.

Advertising has been under severe attack in recent years. While a lot of the criticism has been irresponsible, there are uncomfortably many documented cases of misleading or dishonest advertising. There are other, and more arguable, cases of lapses in good taste. To protect itself, the industry has set up some laudable self-policing procedures, and various government actions have put still further boundaries on what may or may not be done in advertising.

The fact is, though, that there is no generally accepted code of ethical procedures, and probably none could be composed that would erase the problem for all time. The solution lies in the original conception and execution—with the advertiser and the agency acting not as fuzzy corporate structures but as individual, creative, competitive people.

I firmly believe that morals, taste, and responsibility are ingrained traits. Our standards are strongly influenced by environment—by exposure, by example, and to a very high degree by the teaching process. I believe it is as impossible for many men and women to create or approve a vulgar ad or a misleading ad, even were they to be ordered to, as it is impossible for some people to be boorish or to lie or to cheat.

This, clearly, is an area where the college should be able to make a contribution. It is also an area that is likely to be forever blank in the background of the man or woman who comes into advertising out of a purely liberal arts education. It is not enough simply to attain general standards of morality and taste; it is important to be subjected to the deliberate considerations of *advertising* morality and taste, just as it is important for the law student to be exposed to the careful examination of the ethical concepts of the law.

I believe that early and deeply rooted standards of practice are essential to the practitioner of any business or profession if he is to get pride and fulfillment out of his work, not just a living; if he is to be a responsible social and economic innovator, not merely an opportunist. Here, I think, is a clear challenge for the university.

Some of advertising's critics attack it not alone on grounds of morals or taste, but on charges of wastefulness or economics. Its defense has not been handled uniformly well.

Its most vocal supporters, naturally, have been the men and women who live and work in the industry. Only a handful of qualified students and teachers have argued its case, because only a handful have had the time and purpose to make a penetrating study of its value and efficiency.

In the industry, there are many extraordinarily talented creative people who produce advertising that is persuasive, charming, or disarming, yet are struck dumb when they are asked to explain succinctly the economic value of the advertising they create. It is not surprising. They have learned their craft, but they have learned little about how it came into being, why it has grown, and what it really means in a social sense. They are left to plead its case without benefit of prior debate.

By its very character the university has a clear role here. The interdisciplinary opportunities are obvious, and present to a degree and in a diversity the student will never have again. But it is not enough, I think, to send the advertising student across campus to the various survey courses in economics, sociology, psychology, and the like, and then say that he now has the base. If he is to maximize his usefulness to his industry later on, this body of information needs to be brought together and applied to the specifics of advertising. This is a great opportunity, I think, for curriculum development in advertising.

Of course in this area there is need for much more—and much more enlightened—research. Properly, most of the advertising research done by individual media, agencies, or advertisers has been self-oriented. It is, in effect, product research. Very little pure research is going on regarding the validity of the premises on which advertising itself is based. It is axiomatic that stronger teaching programs in advertising will result in stronger basic research. Advanced teaching and advanced research embrace each other.

Let's look now at the area of aesthetics.

Advertising agencies know that if they point their college recruiting efforts toward the student with demonstrated interest in writing and art, they will reduce hiring errors. The American Association of Advertising Agencies has studied successful men and women in the industry, and concluded that working on the college newspaper was, for instance, one point of high correlation among the best advertising people.

If you dig below this rudimentary conclusion, you find that the most successful advertising people, especially in a creative sense, are those who were subjected to the most rigorous writing demands at an early age. My observation further is that where the agency and advertiser training programs fall down most is in the creative and writing area. Only rarely does industry make a creative person out of someone who was not identified as creative before he began working for a living.

To be sure, writing courses are taught outside the advertising curriculum and should be, but the opportunity for concentration should be available to the student who has to write, write, write to be happy. Here, in writing labs, he can be taught the rules, perhaps to be broken later, but with understanding.

But there's much more to it than writing. There is an understanding of the relationship of the visual and verbal, the implantation of tolerance for difference in styles and techniques. It is no longer enough to know how advertising works; it is imperative to understand and be able to choose among the alternative routes of communication.

At the university this is of course being recognized, through the renaming of schools and colleges to group together the totality of the communication process. This is as it should be, and will work counter to the trend toward simply turning out the liberal arts student for a life in advertising or its sister communications services. As the business of advertising becomes the business of communications, the task of on-the-job training is compounded by the necessity to include more and more specialties. Few businesses will be able to keep training programs running long enough to cover the full spectrum.

It seems to me that the total evidence points strongly away from the path advertisers and agencies and our associations have been taking in our relationships with the university. We have promoted gifts to the business schools or to the generalist schools, often at the expense of the department of advertising or the college of communications. We have tried to curry favor with economists and sociologists, to whom advertising is unpalatable, and then, come June, have hunted up the advertising professors for help in hiring their best students.

Dr. Charles Sandage can certainly testify to this. He has probably produced more successful and more responsible advertising men than any teacher who ever lived. Certainly, he has developed more teachers of advertising than anyone else ever has.

He founded the most successful and longest running industry-educator program in existence. He conceived the James Webb Young Fund for advanced students in advertising, and begged his way across the land for enough money to get it going until today it has become the most significant—nearly the only—advanced study program in advertising. He has quietly tried to get a research center started on the basics of advertising here at the University of Illinois, a concept that is bound to come to fulfillment sooner or later.

In fact, Sandy's biggest problem through the years has been that he was consistently ahead of his time. There is almost nothing I have said this evening that Sandy hasn't been saying for years, cornering advertising people at conventions and seminars, tugging at their sleeves, and suggesting that in Champaign-Urbana things were going on in advertising education that they ought to know about. What I have had to say is merely an observation on a fundamental Sandage philosophy.

Sandy has had many honors, elective and appointive, scrolls and bowls, plaques and plaudits. He has books and articles to his credit that will fill advertising bibliographies for years to come.

I'm sure all of these must be satisfying. But if I were Sandy, I think there are two things I would find even more rewarding.

The first is the hundreds of his students and disciples who are keeping and spreading the Sandage faith; who look to him as the man who most influenced their careers.

The second is the inner warmth that must come from knowing that you have made a whole industry better, prouder, and more responsible.

These are frightening times. Of all of the manifestations of unrest and confusion, none is more disturbing than the widespread student rebellions, and none is closer to home for the group of people here.

I have had children in school at Berkeley and Columbia and I have listened to their versions and the versions of their classmates about what these protests really meant. Almost without exception, the student rebellions have been lead by professional revolutionaries such as Mario Savio, Bettina Aptheker, Mark Rudd, and others, some of whom are even second-generation revolutionaries.

The rebellions start round local and sometimes trivial causes, and yet they grow until ultimately some non-revolutionary young people get caught up in them.

For the most part, the students that I have talked to have little sympathy with the leadership, but they are not completely out of sympathy with the root causes that seem to feed the riots. Their complaints have a lot to do with the growing alienation between teacher and student and between student and administration. They find themselves in cynical times taught by cynical teachers in a "mega-university." The human relationship between the student and teacher is missing. The teacher all too often rushes off to his other occupations the minute the lecture is over.

Our young people want leadership, and warmth, and interest, and human involvement. They want to be recognized as individuals. These times cry out for teachers like Dr. Sandage, for teachers who are interested in people as people and in ideals as well as ideas.

This is a significant time to be honoring a career like Sandy's. He is the personification of what our students so desperately want in a teacher.

That's why as Sandy walks among us today he seems a little taller than most of us.

CHAPTER 13

The Role of Advertising Education

by John Crichton

Mr. Crichton is president of the American Association of Advertising Agencies. He previously was editor of Advertising Age *and worked for newspapers in Montana and Colorado. He is secretary and a director of the Advertising Council and a director of the Advertising Research Foundation, American Advertising Federation, and the Traffic Audit Bureau.*

It will be thirty years next fall since I first walked into an advertising class as a college student. It was then a matter of some concern to me that some rather ominous circumstances hung over my chosen field of study.

For instance, it was not certain that if one studied advertising he would ever work in advertising. There was no indication that advertising jobs were being filled either exclusively or even predominantly by people trained in advertising at the college level. The students began, then, with the uneasy knowledge that they might be wasting their time in a vocational sense.

It was also borne in upon the students that many instructors had no formidable credentials of active and successful work in the field of advertising. They feared that they were being taught by people who were more clearly qualified as teachers than as advertising men.

It was also clear from such casual conversations as we were able to arrange with real, live, working advertising men that they distrusted an advertising curriculum, and when pressed for a desirable educational background retreated vaguely to "a good liberal arts education," or "perhaps enough courses in business school to know how to read a balance sheet," or more crisply, "a major in English—lots of writing courses—and a minor in psychology."

Almost to a man, their idea for a good background for advertising was not education in advertising, but a broad education supplemented by, say, retail selling, or door-to-door selling, or perhaps work in a mail-order business. Retailing was to help the tyro advertising man understand people, and how they responded. Mail order was where resultful advertising could be observed, analyzed, and learned.

I mention these personal experiences not because they are relics of the past, more charitably forgotten on this occasion, but because they seem to me to express attitudes which are very nearly as prevalent today as they were 30 years ago, and which have made the relationship between advertising and advertising education such an uneasy partnership.

HAS THE PICTURE CHANGED?

It is probably true today that many of the students who study advertising will probably not work in it—or at least there is no assurance that they will. There is no real indication that the best prospective advertising men are currently enrolled in advertising courses.

What *is* different is that the best of the advertising course graduates now see many recruiters from agencies, advertisers, and media. The effort to hire is much more pronounced, as recruiting has become a way of life for American business.

Times change. The money that graduates from advertising courses can command is impressive. Say, $7,000–$8,000 for a bachelor's degree, $10,000 for a master's. If the student has an M.B.A. from a prestigious graduate business school, the figure is probably $12,000. And it will have doubled in the past decade. This is just a sign of the times. Those of us who remember the thirties remember a very different wage scale— or we have mercifully forgotten it. It was revived for me this spring, in reading *The New Yorker*'s superb reporting of the defense of the British pound in 1964. The key role for the Americans was played by Alfred Hayes, president of the

Federal Reserve Bank of New York. It was revealing to read that Mr. Hayes, who was a Phi Beta Kappa at Yale, and a Rhodes Scholar who wrote a thesis on the Federal Reserve policy and the gold standard, joined New York Trust Co. in 1933, and five years later—the year I began to study advertising—Mr. Hayes was being paid $2,700 a year.

So much for changing times and dollar values. Ideas and attitudes change more slowly.

My second memory of the past was that advertising teachers had not gained impressive reputations as working advertising men. I think this is still true. It may even be a good thing. I'm not sure teaching and working proficiency are the same thing. But, in fact, relatively few of the teachers I know in advertising have behind them any substantial number of years of working at advertising, and even fewer have risen to any particular eminence in advertising.

Third, many advertising men still believe a broad liberal arts background is the most desirable for our business. Advertising teachers have generally said that present curricula tend to give the students far more liberal arts than most of the critics of advertising education seem to realize. But I would hazard the opinion that most advertising men still distrust advertising curricula. I don't know whether the recommendation would still be English and psychology. There is evident a passion for business schools—some agencies attempt to recruit M.B.A.'s *only*. It remains to be seen whether these products turn out to be as promising as their recruitment seems to imply.

One more voice from the past. In 1924—44 years ago, and seven years after the 4A's was founded—Paul T. Cherington reported to the Board of the 4A's on conversations with the National Association of Teachers of Advertising. Mr. Cherington (who was both agency man and college teacher, having taught at Harvard) reported that the teachers wanted summer jobs in agencies for themselves (as refresher experience) and for their students; they also wanted more case histories —more current and usable classroom material. The response of the Board, in those minutes of long ago, was that the agency business was a difficult business in which to utilize part-time or temporary employees, and that case histories were usually confidential and in any case their use would require the cooperation of the client.

For most of my business lifetime, advertising men have complained about advertising education as (1) irrelevant and donnish, or (2) too much like trade-school training in concept to be useful for the broad needs of the business.

Advertising educators have complained that (1) they were individually unappreciated; (2) that their efforts were singularly lacking in business support; and (3) they represented beacheads on a hostile intellectual shore, and were never properly recognized for their valor and dedication. All of which is probably true.

Advertising has been taught on college campuses for more than 50 years. I am now drawing largely on Dr. Sandage's definitive article in *Printers' Ink*, in June, 1963.

The first wave of college interest in advertising came in the first decade of this century, and was marked by such luminaries as Dr. Harlow Gale at Minnesota, Dr. Walter Dill Scott at Northwestern, Dr. Daniel Starch at Wisconsin, and Dr. H. F. Adams at Michigan. The first course in advertising at the college level was offered by the University of Missouri in 1908, followed by the University of Washington in 1910, and the University of Wisconsin in 1913. All courses were offered as part of the school or department of journalism. New York University had an extension course in 1905, Wharton School at the University of Pennsylvania offered a course in 1910, Illinois in 1914, and Harvard—through Paul Cherington —in 1916. Daniel Starch was to take over as Harvard's teacher, having pioneered at Wisconsin. Starch was succeeded at Harvard by Neil Borden. Dr. Starch was for a time research director for the 4A's, and went on to do notable work in readership research.

At this point, there are more than 500 colleges where some advertising courses are offered, and about 35 where an advertising major is possible.

We owe a debt of gratitude to the teachers of advertising. They made advertising a respectable course of study. They have persevered in improving its teaching with a modicum of encouragement or support. Yet there is a flaw even in this particular piece of acknowledgment and confession. The business isn't geared very closely to these academic efforts.

This ends the preface. Now comes the research.

THE EDUCATION OF TOP AGENCY EXECUTIVES

We, the 4A's, are often asked, "How should advertising be taught?" We have stubbornly said that education is the province of the educator—and our task is to help him.

We are also asked, "What is the best background for advertising?" or, alternatively, "What is the background most advertising men have?" These are, of course, different questions. I cannot answer what is the best background. I can tell you something about what the educational backgrounds of present agency people are.

I make an immediate concession. It is recognized that agencies are only part of the advertising business, and even a fairly small part, numerically. We sent a questionnaire to 465 individual agency people in 48 offices of 31 larger agencies across the country. We do not claim that our sample is representative of the agency business in the United States; we do believe it is representative of individuals in larger A.A.A.A. agencies, including branch offices.

For the management group we surveyed chairmen of the board, vice-chairmen, presidents, chairmen of executive committees, and executive vice-presidents. For creative people— people called "creative director." For research and media —the top research and media title. For marketing and contact —the head of the department. All told, we had 362 returns. That's 78 per cent of the sample.

In Table 1 are summarized the results for 322 of the 362 individuals whom we could classify by job function.

This table tells you that there are few doctoral degrees in our business, and that most of them are in media and research. Master's degrees are fairly minor among executive and creative types, quite common in media and research, and in contact and marketing about one man in five has one.

In Table 1 you may note the high percentages who attended graduate school but got no degree. Combining the figures for undergraduate degrees and graduate work but no degree one

TABLE 1: LEVEL OF EDUCATION

	TOTAL	EXECUTIVE	CREATIVE	MEDIA/ RESEARCH	CONTACT/ MARKETING
	(322)	(107)	(93)	(75)	(47)
Doctoral Degree	2%	2%	0%	4%	0%
Master's Degree	15	8	4	33	19
Graduate—No Degree	16	15	14	19	15
Undergraduate Degree Only	43	54	42	29	45
Undergraduate— No Degree	13	13	18	8	15
Did Not Attend College	11	8	22	7	6
Total	100%	100%	100%	100%	100%

arrives at about 60 per cent. The media and research group is the best formally educated group in the agency business. Table 1 also discloses a fairly substantial group who attended but did not graduate from college. It shows also that one person in nine did not go to college. Note that among top creative people 40 per cent—that's almost half—either did not go to or did not complete college.

Executive Group

I should now like to examine the executive group.

TABLE 2: EXECUTIVE GROUP

	TOTAL	UP TO 49	50 AND OVER
Doctoral Degree	2 (2%)	2 (4%)	0 (0%)
Master's Degree	9 (8)	6 (13)	3 (5)
Graduate—No Degree	16 (15)	8 (17)	8 (14)
Undergraduate Degree Only	58 (54)	25 (52)	33 (56)
Undergraduate— No Degree	13 (13)	3 (6)	10 (17)
Did Not Attend College	9 (8)	4 (8)	5 (8)
Total	107 (100%)	48 (100%)	59 (100%)

Of the 107 agency top executives, only two have doctorates. Both are under 49. Of the nine who have master's, six are under 49. Those who attended graduate school but did not graduate are evenly divided between age groups. There are markedly fewer who did not graduate from college in the younger group.

Where did they go to undergraduate college?

TABLE 3: EXECUTIVE GROUP—UNDERGRADUATE SCHOOLS

	TOTAL	UP TO 49	50 AND OVER
	(98)	(44)	(54)
Private Eastern	63 (64%)	30 (68%)	33 (59%)
Private Midwestern	11 (11)	5 (11)	6 (11)
Private Western	1 (1)	0 (0)	1 (2)
State Eastern	5 (5)	4 (9)	1 (2)
State Midwestern	26 (26)	10 (23)	16 (30)
State Western	2 (2)	2 (5)	0 (0)
Foreign	3 (3)	1 (2)	2 (4)

About two-thirds went to a private eastern college and a little more than a fourth went to a midwestern state university. Totals are higher than 100 per cent because some went to more than one school. The state midwestern percentage drops somewhat among the younger executives.

Because the two types of schools came up so strongly, we have broken them down into the individual colleges.

TABLE 4: EXECUTIVE GROUP—PRIVATE EASTERN UNDER-GRADUATE SCHOOLS

Yale	14	Fordham	1
Princeton	6	Washington &	
Harvard	6	Lee	1
Dartmouth	6	Carnegie Tech	1
Columbia	5	Franklin &	
NYU	4	Marshall	1
Pittsburgh	3	Colgate	1
Cornell	2	St. John's	1
Syracuse	2	Drew	1
Pennsylvania	1	Spring Hill	1
Brown	1	Williams	1
Lehigh	1	Pratt	1
Amherst	1	Millsaps	1

Yale produced more executives than any other two eastern schools combined. Princeton, Harvard, Dartmouth, and Columbia are in a group, followed by NYU, Pittsburgh, Cornell, Syracuse, and 15 other private colleges.

TABLE 5: EXECUTIVE GROUP—STATE MIDWESTERN UNDER-GRADUATE SCHOOLS

Michigan	5	Indiana	1
Michigan State	3	Indiana State	1
Minnesota	3	Ohio State	1
Illinois	3	Nebraska	1
Wisconsin	2	Kansas	1
Missouri	2	Wayne State	1
Purdue	2		

Among state universities, Michigan is the leader, followed closely by Michigan State, Minnesota, Illinois, Wisconsin, Missouri, Purdue, and six other state institutions.

That's where they went. What did they study?

TABLE 6: EXECUTIVE GROUP—UNDERGRADUATE MAJOR

	TOTAL	UP TO 49	50 AND OVER
English	31 (32%)	14 (32%)	17 (31%)
Economics	19 (19)	6 (14)	13 (24)
Business Administration	10 (10)	4 (9)	6 (11)
Journalism	10 (10)	3 (7)	7 (13)
History	8 (8)	4 (9)	4 (7)
Psychology	6 (6)	4 (9)	2 (4)
Political Science	6 (6)	0 (0)	6 (11)
Engineering	5 (5)	3 (7)	2 (4)
Advertising	4 (4)	0 (0)	4 (7)
Liberal Arts	4 (4)	1 (2)	3 (6)
Mathematics	4 (4)	1 (2)	3 (6)
Marketing	3 (3)	1 (2)	2 (4)
Sociology	2 (2)	0 (0)	2 (4)
Philosophy	2 (2)	1 (2)	1 (2)
Science	2 (2)	0 (0)	2 (4)
International	2 (2)	2 (5)	0 (0)

(6 other subjects mentioned once)

English—economics—business administration—journalism—history. Advertising and marketing are well down the list, and both did better with older executives than younger ones. I believe the only real significance of this table is that it tends to make clear why so many advertising men say that subjects in the "liberal arts" are the desired and desirable background for advertising. It clearly is *their* background.

Now about graduate school.

TABLE 7: EXECUTIVE GROUP—GRADUATE SCHOOLS

	TOTAL	UP TO 49	50 AND OVER
	(27)	(16)	(11)
Private Eastern	14 (52%)	8 (50%)	6 (55%)
Private Midwestern	6 (22)	3 (19)	3 (27)
Private Western	0 (0)	0 (0)	0 (0)
State Eastern	2 (7)	1 (6)	1 (9)
State Midwestern	3 (11)	2 (13)	1 (9)
State Western	3 (11)	3 (19)	0 (0)
Foreign	2 (7)	1 (6)	1 (9)

Graduate students chose private graduate schools over state schools. Younger men are more likely to have gone to graduate school.

Here are the private eastern schools and principal midwestern schools.

TABLE 8: EXECUTIVE GROUP—GRADUATE SCHOOLS

PRIVATE EASTERN		PRIVATE MIDWESTERN	
Columbia	5	Northwestern	4
Harvard	3	Chicago	2
Dartmouth	2		
Yale	2		
Syracuse	1		
Clark	1		

What did they study in graduate school?

TABLE 9: EXECUTIVE GROUP—GRADUATE MAJOR

	TOTAL	UP TO 49	50 AND OVER
	(27)	(16)	(11)
Marketing	8 (30%)	5 (31%)	3 (27%)
Economics	3 (11)	2 (13)	1 (9)
English	2 (7)	2 (13)	0 (0)
Law	2 (7)	0 (0)	2 (18)

Once: Engineering   Motion Picture Production   Retailing
         Finance   Classics   Advertising
         History   Statistics   Management
         Architecture   Business   Diplomatic Service

They studied everything. Marketing emerged as important here. Some fields mentioned once were architecture, retailing, advertising, the classics, and motion picture production.

We asked about special technical training. About one in ten executives—10 percent—had some special training of some kind. Advertising and art are mentioned here, and so are accounting and French.

What does our survey tell us? First, that most of the executives went to or graduated from college; that many of the younger men in the group went to graduate school; that a noticeable proportion did not go to college, and the proportion is fairly constant. We've seen that the most consistently and best educated are the research and media group, and that the creative group is notably free from formal education.

I do not intend to present four groups with the same detail just accorded the executive group. I would, however, like to illustrate the differences between the groups with some tables and brief comments.

Creative Group

Now for the group of 93 creative people.

TABLE 10: CREATIVE GROUP

	TOTAL	UP TO 49	50 AND OVER
Doctoral Degree	0 (0%)	0 (0%)	0 (0%)
Master's Degree	4 (4)	3 (4)	1 (3)
Graduate—No Degree	13 (14)	11 (17)	2 (7)
Undergraduate Degree Only	39 (42)	33 (51)	6 (21)
Undergraduate—No Degree	17 (18)	7 (11)	10 (37)
Did Not Attend College	20 (22)	11 (17)	9 (32)
Total	93 (100%)	65 (100%)	28 (100%)

There were no doctoral degrees, and only 4 of the 93 people had master's degrees. I noted before that 40 per cent of the people in this group either did not attend or did not graduate from college. You can see from this table, though, that there is a markedly greater degree of formal education among the younger group, not only in absolute numbers, but also on a percentage basis.

Where did they go to undergraduate college?

TABLE 11: CREATIVE GROUP—UNDERGRADUATE SCHOOLS

	TOTAL	UP TO 49	50 AND OVER
	(73)	(54)	(19)
Private Eastern	44 (60%)	31 (56%)	13 (68%)
Private Midwestern	17 (23)	12 (22)	5 (26)
Private Western	4 (5)	3 (6)	1 (5)
State Eastern	7 (10)	7 (13)	0 (0)
State Midwestern	9 (12)	8 (15)	1 (5)
State Western	8 (11)	7 (13)	1 (5)

Again, a high percentage attended a private eastern school, but in general the group shows much more of a spread than did the executive group. This is especially true of the younger people.

What did they study?

TABLE 12: CREATIVE GROUP—UNDERGRADUATE MAJOR

	TOTAL	UP TO 49	50 AND OVER
	(73)	(54)	(19)
English	30 (41%)	16 (30%)	14 (74%)
Art and Design	11 (15)	6 (11)	5 (26)
Advertising and Marketing	8 (11)	6 (11)	2 (11)
Journalism	8 (11)	8 (15)	0 (0)
Drama	4 (5)	4 (7)	0 (0)
History	4 (5)	4 (7)	0 (0)
Economics	2 (3)	1 (2)	1 (5)
Philosophy	2 (3)	1 (2)	1 (5)
Music	2 (3)	1 (2)	1 (5)
Business Administration	2 (3)	1 (2)	1 (5)
Once:	Fashion		German
	Communications		Theology
	Biology		

English, art and design, advertising and marketing, journalism all show up strongly, as might be expected. But there are still a considerable number of people from widely varying backgrounds, from fashion to biology to theology. Before going on to the next group, I should point out that 31 per cent of the creative people attended some type of specialized or technical school—about three times that of any of the other groups. Art and copy were the predominant subjects.

Media and Research Group

Let's look at the best formally educated group in the agency business, the media and research group.

TABLE 13: MEDIA/RESEARCH GROUP

	TOTAL	UP TO 49	50 AND OVER
Doctoral Degree	3 (4%)	3 (5%)	0 (0%)
Master's Degree	25 (33)	21 (36)	4 (24)
Graduate—No Degree	14 (19)	11 (19)	3 (18)
Undergraduate Degree Only	22 (29)	17 (30)	5 (29)
Undergraduate—No Degree	6 (8)	4 (7)	2 (11)
Did Not Attend College	5 (7)	2 (3)	3 (18)
Total	75 (100%)	58 (100%)	17 (100%)

Seventy-five people reported in this group, and 42 of them—56 per cent—had some formal education beyond undergraduate school. Twenty-eight (37 per cent) received graduate degrees. Again the younger group shows more formal education than the older group.

Where did they go to school?

TABLE 14: MEDIA/RESEARCH GROUP—UNDERGRADUATE SCHOOLS

	TOTAL	UP TO 49	50 AND OVER
	(70)	(56)	(14)
Private Eastern	33 (47%)	27 (48%)	6 (43%)
Private Midwestern	14 (20)	9 (16)	5 (36)
Private Western	3 (4)	2 (4)	1 (7)
State Eastern	15 (21)	14 (25)	1 (7)
State Midwestern	13 (19)	11 (20)	2 (14)
State Western	5 (7)	3 (5)	2 (14)

The distribution of schools is noticeably more spread out than it is for the executive group. Private eastern and midwestern schools and state eastern and midwestern schools all show up fairly strongly.

What did they study?

Advertising and marketing are at the top of the list for the first time, followed by psychology, English, journalism, and mathematics. The graduate school majors of this group also show advertising and marketing at the top, with psychology

**TABLE 15: MEDIA/RESEARCH GROUP—UNDERGRADUATE
            MAJOR**

	TOTAL	UP TO 49	50 AND OVER
	(70)	(56)	(14)
Advertising and Marketing	14 (20%)	12 (21%)	2 (14%)
Psychology	10 (14)	8 (14)	2 (14)
English	9 (13)	6 (11)	3 (21)
Journalism	7 (10)	7 (12)	0 (0)
Mathematics and Statistics	7 (10)	6 (11)	1 (7)
Economics	5 (7)	2 (4)	3 (21)
Business	5 (7)	2 (4)	3 (21)
History	5 (7)	5 (10)	0 (0)
Engineering	3 (4)	2 (4)	1 (7)
Once:	Accounting		Geology
	Fine Arts		Science

and business second and third. Besides being the best formally
educated group, the media and research group also shows the
greatest concentration in advertising and marketing and related majors.

Marketing and Account Service Group

The final group includes marketing directors and account
service people.

TABLE 16: CONTACT/MARKETING GROUP

	TOTAL	UP TO 49	50 AND OVER
Doctoral Degree	0 (0%)	0 (0%)	0 (0%)
Master's Degree	9 (19)	8 (22)	1 (10)
Graduate—No Degree	7 (15)	6 (16)	1 (10)
Undergraduate Degree Only	21 (45)	14 (38)	7 (70)
Undergraduate—No Degree	7 (15)	6 (16)	1 (10)
Did Not Attend College	3 (6)	3 (8)	0 (0)
Total	47 (100%)	37 (100%)	10 (100%)

Forty-seven people are in this group, and only 10 of them are
aged 50 or over. This low number makes comparisons between
the two age groups difficult, although 14 of the 16 people
who attended graduate school or received a graduate degree
were under 50. The total for this group shows a marked
similarity to the executive group, with one exception—there

are about twice as many graduate degrees in this group on a percentage basis.

Where did they go to undergraduate school?

TABLE 17: CONTACT/MARKETING GROUP—UNDERGRADUATE SCHOOLS

	TOTAL	UP TO 49	50 AND OVER
	(44)	(34)	(10)
Private Eastern	25 (57%)	21 (62%)	4 (40%)
Private Midwestern	13 (30)	8 (24)	5 (50)
Private Western	1 (2)	1 (3)	0 (0)
State Eastern	1 (2)	1 (3)	0 (0)
State Midwestern	9 (20)	8 (24)	1 (10)
State Western	9 (20)	7 (21)	2 (20)

Private eastern still heads the list with 25 of the 44 respondents. For the first time, state western schools register a significant percentage. Private and state midwestern schools also show substantial percentages.

What did they study?

TABLE 18: CONTACT/MARKETING GROUP—UNDERGRADUATE MAJOR

	TOTAL	UP TO 49	50 AND OVER
	(44)	(34)	(10)
Advertising and Marketing	10 (23%)	9 (26%)	1 (10%)
Economics	7 (16)	5 (15)	2 (20)
Business Administration	5 (11)	4 (12)	1 (10)
English	5 (11)	2 (6)	3 (30)
Journalism	4 (9)	3 (9)	1 (10)
Political Science	4 (9)	4 (12)	0 (0)
Psychology	2 (5)	2 (6)	0 (0)
Mathematics	2 (5)	2 (6)	0 (0)
History	2 (5)	0 (0)	1 (20)

Once:	Sociology	Geology
	Architecture	Market Research

Advertising and marketing again top the list, followed by economics, business, English, journalism, and political science, then psychology, mathematics, and history with 2 each, and four other subjects mentioned once.

These results are difficult to generalize. It is clear that some parts of the agency business are showing pronounced gains in graduate education. Some of the people with graduate degrees will work their way into the management group of advertising agencies. It may be worth remarking that geography clearly plays a major part in the results of this analysis. If you grew up in the Midwest, it is more likely that you attended a state school, and more likely that you majored in advertising. The tradition of the liberal arts college is grounded in the East—although there are eminent liberal arts institutions throughout the country—and most graduates of eastern schools who work in agencies were liberal arts majors.

Creative people tend to be less formally educated. Why is this so? Impatience? The feeling that the college can instill many skills and disciplines, but that creativity is not one of them? I ask the question; I do not have the answer. I suspect that—considering the importance of the creative man and the creative product in our business—it would be well worth knowing more about.

Finally, there is the substantial block of management men who did not go to college. You will remember that the dividing line in age was 50. This is in part because few men reach management below 35, and for purposes of this study it was more meaningful to use that breaking point. You'll remember that the percentages are about the same in the younger group as in the older group.

I think it is important to emphasize here that the agency business tends to be an entrepreneurial business. It is worth remarking that of the ten largest advertising agencies, seven still have one of the founders living, and in six of them at least one of the founders is still active in the business. This important element of entrepreneurship is cited because, it seems to me, entrepreneurs share with the creative men some of the impatience with existing institutions—and, in the agency business, the creative man and the entrepreneur are frequently the same person.

Recent Agency-Educator Programs

I now leave the research and I would like to look briefly at some recent developments. For the last dozen years, the

Central Region of the 4A's has conducted a program with teachers of advertising in the Midwest, which includes campus visits by agency task forces and summer fellowships for teachers to work within agencies.

This program owes its origin to Dr. Sandage and to Earle Ludgin. It has been copied and adapted elsewhere. At a typical Central Region meeting in Chicago we are likely to have as many as 60 advertising educators as our guests. It has been a mutually beneficial experience.

I'm sure you know that Dr. Sandage is a member of the academic committee for the A.A.A.A. Educational Foundation. A little more than a year ago we announced the establishment of this Foundation. It is intended to add to the body of knowledge about advertising, to increase interest in advertising as a career, to create a better bridge to the campus, and a better understanding of advertising among students and educators, working primarily at the graduate level. The foundation will make grants for research into advertising, marketing, communications, and consumer behavior.

The first grants, 11 in all, totaling $102,243 for the first year, were awarded recently. They went to universities all across the country. They covered subjects ranging from computer models to physiological devices for measuring creative work to communicating with the urban poor. They went to a distinguished group of researchers. The number and quality of research proposals in answer to our announcement was gratifying—and a little overwhelming. The award winners were about evenly divided between graduate business schools and graduate schools in other disciplines.

This university received a grant, and one of this university's professors, working with a professor from a great West Coast university, shared another. It is still too early to be very definite about the Foundation and what it can be expected to do. Quite clearly it offers the opportunity for people who are interested in researching some aspect of advertising to find funds to accomplish that research. It is our expectation that these findings will prove useful both on the campus and off— in the advertising business, and perhaps even with government. The research literature of advertising is not extensive. Its formal application to our business has not been widely beneficial because much of it is privately done, is proprietary in nature, and is secret because it was done for clients and in many cases is their property.

We hope that from these research grants to universities will come information that is useful to the advertising business, to the university, and to people who will work in both. We hope that the grants will help to equip people better to work in advertising, to understand advertising, and to make decisions about advertising. We hope to attract bright research minds to the study of our business, and that they will serve both the university and our business—as indeed has Dr. Sandage during his remarkable career.

SUMMARY

In the course of this paper, I have tried to outline some problems and approaches. One clear-cut problem in the uneasy partnership of advertising and education is that advertising men are far from agreed about what constitutes a superior background for the business of advertising. The research I showed you testifies to the varied backgrounds of the present managerial group in advertising agencies. I would not expect this situation to change. It might be more convenient from an educational standpoint if all advertising men had the same background, but I suspect in reality that it is better that they do not. Our business benefits from the varied backgrounds brought to it.

The 4A's has taken the historical position that what an educator teaches is his province. We don't attempt to tell him what or how to teach. We are willing to help him with any material which may be useful to him; to try to put information, advertising experience, and people at his disposal. It is not a position to be lightly changed. Yet, as new colleges are formed, and new kinds of colleges come into operation, we are confronted with many inquiries about model curricula. It could very well be that a joint educator-practitioner task force could work in this area.

Finally, we have begun a program of inquiry into the improvement of advertising and its understanding through research grants. We have said from the beginning that we hoped this activity would be widely supported. We would cheerfully change the name of the A.A.A.A. Educational Foundation to something more catholic if donors were to appear from other parts of the advertising business. I hope they will, and I hope that as the years go on, the Foundation will play an important part in giving educators who are interested in advertising as a subject—and our hope is that they will be many and from all academic disciplines—an opportunity to study, analyze, and improve advertising's theory and practice.

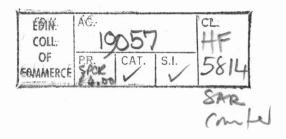